COMPENDIUM OF FAIRIES

OTHERWORLDLY ORACLE

COPYRIGHT 2023

WRITTEN & COMPILED BY KITTY FIELDS

For Otherworldly Oracle

Contents

Foreword 4

Part I: Fairy Lore and Legend 6

   The Fae Folk: A Primer 7

   Are Fairies Real? Origins and Evidence that Fairies Exist 15

   Types of Fairies Worldwide 20

   Types of Mermaids Worldwide 34

   Elementals and the Guardians of the Watchtowers 47

   The Irish Banshee and Leanan sidhe 52

   Kelpies: Mystical Celtic WATER Horse 57

   Fairies in America: Fairy Lore and Sightings 66

   Fairy Changelings: Taken by the Fairies 74

   Household Fairies & Elves 79

   The Green Man Legend 86

   The Connection Between Fairies and Witches 93

   Mermen: Old Legends, Gods, and Sightings 100

   King of the Fairies, Knockma Hill, and a Haunted Castle Hackett 106

Part II: Fairy Magick and Mischief 115

   Attract Fairies To Your Home & Garden 116

   Fairy Foods: What DO Fairies Eat? 122

   Household Spirits: How to Feed and Care For Them 130

   How to Find a Fairy In Your House 137

   Fairy Knot Magic: A Witch's Ladder 144

   Fairy Potions: Magical Fay Elixirs for All 4 Seasons 146

   Protection from Trickster Fairies 151

Bibliography 156

Foreword

When I started the Otherworldly Oracle blog, it was 2018 and I was just coming out of a decades-long relationship with a popular writing platform. I won't name names. It turns out, they were being deceitful in more ways than one. I knew I had to make a change, and fortunately, I randomly ran into an incredibly successful blogger who inspired me and encouraged me to go out on a limb and start my own witchy blog. When I decided to remove all my blog posts from said writing platform, the higher-ups told me I would "never be as successful on my own" and that I would "regret leaving" their platform. Well, I don't take too kindly to comments like these. The more someone tells me I can't do something, the more I want to prove them wrong. And it turns out, it was the best business decision I'd ever made.

After I left the platform, I published OtherworldlyOracle.com and moved hundreds of my blog posts to my new website. Over the past 5 years, I've written till my fingers bled, invited amazing guest bloggers to share their thoughts and stories on the site, and I had the pleasure of co-founding the Otherworldly Oracle Official Podcast with my witchy sister Allorah Rayne. Shout out to Allorah for years of magical friendship, for putting up with my daily crap, and for giving me the idea to compile all my blog posts into books!

Amazingly, and with help from my loyal readers, I've watched the blog and podcast grow in popularity and I've been told how helpful it has been for those on unique and pagan spiritual journeys. I couldn't have done it without you! With this Compendium of Fairies, I hope to provide my readers with a physical copy of the Otherworldly Oracle Fairies Archives.

Currently, I have published three books for Otherworldly Oracle including Modern Witchcraft: A Beginner's No-nonsense Guide to the Craft, The Otherworldly Household: A No-nonsense Guide to Enchanting the Witch's Home, and Otherworldly Oracle's Compendium of Pagan Gods. There is much more to come!

Please be on the look-out for upcoming Otherworldly Oracle Compendiums which will compile the website's archives on Seasons and Sabbats, Spells and Rituals, Kitchen Witchcraft, Ghosts, and more. Listen into the Otherworldly Oracle Official Podcast on your preferred podcast app. Follow Otherworldly Oracle on FaceBook, Instagram, and Pinterest. If you'd like exclusive content and have access to my apprenticeship program called Traditions, join me on Patreon at Patreon.com/OtherworldlyOracle. And remember, stay otherworldly!

Part I: Fairy Lore and Legend

The Fae Folk: A Primer

There's a world parallel to ours, or perhaps underneath. Or maybe somewhere in-betwixt. It's a world in the mist, under and beyond the sea, filled with beings not unlike us. And yet somehow, they're completely different. I'm talking about the fairy realm. The fae folk reside there. Have you ever wanted to meet the fae? In this blog post, take an enchanted journey with me to their world and learn of their origins, their true nature, their likes, and dislikes, and basically everything we know about them. Enjoy meeting them, but don't eat the food! Or you might not ever return to our world.

Since I was a little girl, I've been obsessed with the fae. Fairy tales like Thumbelina, The Little Mermaid, and Rumpelstiltskin fed my belief in another world parallel to ours…the world of the fae. When I was nine years old, a family member gave me a roleplaying board game called Tales of the Crystals. Of which further fueled my desire to learn more about fairies and even be more like fairies. During my teen years, I began studying fairy lore and I haven't turned back since.

The Fae Folk: Who Are They, Exactly?

So, who are the fae folk, exactly? If you haven't figured it out by now, the words fae and fae folk are just other names for fairies. You've surely seen them in movies or in books, haven't you? The thing is, they're often portrayed as beautiful, winged pixies flitting from flower top to flower top. Hollywood has painted a picture of the fae that is deceitful at worst, narrow-minded at best. Because the true nature of the fae is incredibly complex. And not all fae are cute little pixies.

Classification: The Seelie and Unseelie Courts

The nature of the fae folk can't be divided into strict categories like good and bad. Some cultures have tried to label them and define them. In Scottish and Northern English folklore, the Seelie Court is the "mostly good, benevolent" fairies. While the Unseelie Court is made up of harmful fairies that tend to be malevolent towards humans more so than the Seelie Court. Fun fact! The word Seelie means happy or lucky and is the word from which silly is derived. So, when someone says you're acting silly, you can smile and know you've just been called a fairy!

But to continue defining the fae folk, we'd have to call them both good and bad. They are an oxymoron. A divine paradox. Because even though the Scottish called the Seelie mostly benevolent, they still considered them dangerous to humans. This is because fairies don't adhere to human rules. They don't follow our logic on ethics or morals. They have their own set of rules they go by, which on this plane of existence might seem very "gray".

The Capriciousness of the Fae

The fae folk enjoy playing tricks on humans. It seems no matter the type or class of fairy, they are capricious at their core. Even the Scottish household fae, the Brownie, will turn malevolent towards humans if angered. He will play nasty tricks on his house and all who live in it. And those cute little pixies that drop fairy dust behind them? While they can be helpful to deserving individuals, they're also known to pinch and kick lazy humans. Or anyone they feel like.

"Provided that you didn't interfere with 'em, they wouldn't say or do anything to you." ~ Green and Lenihan's "Meeting the Other Crowd"

But What Are They? Fallen Angels? Tiny Humans? Or Spirits?

Now that we've established the fae are mischievous and have their own set of rules, let's answer the question what are the fae? This is an even harder question to answer. There have been dozens of theories put forth over the centuries. One theory says the fae are fallen angels, spirits that are stuck between Heaven and Hell. Another says the fae are the souls of unbaptized babies, not good enough to ascend but not bad enough to burn for eternity.

Another theory says the fae are actual physical beings – a race of smaller human beings that evolved to fit their habitat. In 2003, archaeologists found a race of dwarf-sized human beings they named homo floriensis of which they also called hobbits. The female skeleton stood under a meter tall with her head the "size of a grapefruit", according to Wired.com. Homo floriensis lived only 18,000 years ago. Taking this information into account, isn't it possible a similar race of small human beings might have lived elsewhere on the planet, spurring beliefs in fairies?

While I'm inclined to scientifically rationalize and adhere to the previous theory, my magical self thinks the fae folk are more complicated than that. Many people today still believe in the fae, and that instead of being lost souls or fallen angels. Or even a race of small human beings, the fae folk are spiritual in nature. They are liminal creatures, meaning they can manifest in the physical but they are ethereal in form. And if they are truly spiritual beings, this means they can shapeshift and take nearly any form they choose. They could be giants or tiny pixies. A water-logged, majestic water horse like the kelpie or a hideous, human-eating troll under a bridge. They could even take the form of our worst fears or most beautiful dreams.

The fae folk may also be a type of guardian spirit called an elemental. Elementals are spirits of nature – the actual consciousness of the land, trees, rivers, mountains, etc. Perhaps the fae are simply that – nature spirits. But again, I think there's much more to the fae than meets the eye.

<u>Where to Find The Fae Folk</u>

Maybe you've seen a fairy before. Or maybe you're dying to see one in real life. I can't guarantee you'll ever see one of the fae. Because, let's face it, they're elusive, finicky little things. If they want you to see them, you will. If they don't want you to see them, you won't. It's as simple as that. However, it may be possible to find them at their sacred haunts, typically in natural, untouched places. They are frequently felt, heard and seen in the forests, playing in and around creeks and rivers, on the tops of mountains, and near waterfalls. Although, I have a friend who claims he's seen one smack-dab in the middle of a crowded city. Remember when I said there are no rules with the fae? They could be anywhere.

Fairy Rings and Trails

A particularly well-known sign a fairy is near is the fairy ring. Fairy rings are light or dark colored circles in the grass, a circle of mushrooms, or even a small circle of stones. You're likely to find that a small circle of stones created by fairies will be in a forest, far away from human hustle and bustle. But fairy rings of the grass or mushroom variety? You might see those in your own backyard! They say you should never stop into the middle of a fairy ring, lest you be whisked away to the fairy realm forever. The fairy trail or path is "like a faery ring except it's a long trail of dark grass rather than a circle", according to the late author and witch Edain McCoy. She says these fairy trails are the roads that trooping fairies take to travel from one place to the next.

Fairy Mounds

In Ireland, we have something called fairy mounds. Also called fairy forts or raths. These are essentially ruins of old Medieval forts but can also be hills or ancient burial mounds. For centuries, at least since the late Medieval Age, the people believed these hills to be the dwellings of the fae folk. Many sightings tell of fairies entering and emerging from fairy mounds. These mounds are portals or doors to the fairy realm. Irish lore says never to disturb a fairy fort – even cutting trees or bushes that surround the fairy fort may warrant the individual's untimely death.

Interestingly, there seems to be some overlap between the fae and ancient ancestors. Some of the burial mounds where we've found human remains are also associated with the fae. And still some mythical figures in Ireland, like Queen Medb for example, are purportedly buried in a fairy mound. And with Queen Medb specifically, she crosses over from mythical queen to fairy queen to goddess. So, it begs to question, were the fairies our ancestors' spirits or vice versa? But I don't want to confuse you, so let's keep talking about places to find fairies.

The Celtic Otherworld

In Celtic mythology, there's another place parallel to ours, or sometimes underneath ours, called the Otherworld. The fae folk are often featured in myths about the Otherworld. In the Silver Gadelica, Teigue takes a journey across the sea (an Immramma) and meets the fairy queen Cliodhna in the Celtic Otherworld. In fact, many of the myths about the Celtic Otherworld tell us that it's a land through the mist and/or across the ocean. And that it's often a place made up of many mystical islands…like earth yet different. It's a beautiful place, and sometimes a terrifying place, filled with wonders, healing trees, and fairies. But it can also prove dangerous and be a horrible place filled with monsters. This truly depends on the myth and whose journey it is. Many believe the Celtic Otherworld is also where we go when we die.

"Bran sees the number of waves beating across the clear sea: I myself sea Mag Mon, Red headed flowers without fault. Sea-horses glisten in the summer, as far as Bran has stretched his glance: rivers pour forth a stream of honey, in the land of Manannan son of Ler." ~ The Voyage of Bran mac Febal to the Land of the Living, circa 900 AD

Faeries In the Home

It might surprise you to learn the fae folk sometimes make their home in OUR homes. Yes, there are fairies who prefer to take up a cozy bed in a nice family's abode. I call these household fairies, and they are typically benevolent to humans. For the most part. Unless they are angered. Household fairies are said to live in an undisturbed, quite cabinet, cupboard, or closet somewhere in the house. Some live in, under or behind the hearth, like the Slavic Domovoi. There are even fairies who live in the wine cellar, in the barn, and in other inconspicuous places. They tend to come out at night when we are all asleep and do their work.

Signs the Fae Folk Are Near

How do you know when they're present? Or even near? Here's some signs to watch for:

- Hearing far-off music, specifically harps and flutes
- Things go missing or get moved without explanation (particularly shiny things like jewelry, rings, coins, trinkets, crystals, etc.)
- Your garden is thriving! Flowers are blooming earlier than expected OR seem to have burst forth overnight
- Finding a fairy ring in your garden or yard
- If a mess has been made of the straw in your garden or barn (faeries love to play in the straw)

- You find fairy knots in your hair OR in your animals hair
- Seeing them in your dreams or during a hypnogogic state
- Leaving offerings and finding them gone the next day (bowl is empty, cup licked clean, etc.)
- Finding your kitchen or home cleaner than when you left it (if we should all be so blessed!)

Books on Fairies (And Sources Used):

A Witch's Guide to Faery Folk by Edain McCoy

The Fairy-Faith in Celtic Countries by WY Evans Wentz

Fairy and Folk Tales of the Irish Peasantry by WB Yeats

Meeting the Other Crowd by Eddie Lenihan & Carolyn Eve Green

Tales of the Celtic Otherworld by John Matthews

Are Fairies Real? Origins and Evidence that Fairies Exist

Many people want to know if fairies are real. Fairies have been a central figure of legends for hundreds of years. Today we know fairies mostly by what we see on the TV or in books, but at one time our ancestors believed fairies were part of daily life. Think about it like this – legends might seem elaborate and fantastical, but they stem from some truth. Whether the truth has been diluted or transformed over the years, there is some truth to the belief in fairies. Let's explore potential evidence of fairy existence together.

What Are Fairies? Fallen Gods?

Perhaps the answer to our questions about fairies lies in their origins. In Ireland, some say the fairies are fallen gods known as the Tuatha de Danann. The name translates to "people of Danu, the Mother Goddess". These Ancient gods and goddesses were said to live underground in a separate realm. This belief corresponds with the idea that fairies enter and exit our world through hills called fairy mounds. The Church demonized the old gods and goddesses by turning them into less-powerful spirits. The common-folk's fairy traditions were outlawed by the Church.

Are They Nature Spirits or Lost Souls?

Another possibility is that fairies are simply nature spirits. The French folklorist Claude Lecouteux theorizes that fairies are guardians of natural places like rivers, trees, mountains, hills, and more. They are the spirits of place that sometimes manifest in physical form like pixies, dragons, mermaids, gnomes, dwarves, and elves. If you believe everything in nature has consciousness, then this theory aligns quite well.

A Medieval oral tradition maintains that fairies are the souls of lost pagans who died before the word of Christ could reach them. To expand or change this idea slightly, others said fairies are the souls of unbaptized children trapped between this world and the next. Not bad enough to go to Hell, yet not good enough to go to Heaven. Caught in some kind of purgatory.

An Ingrained Ancestral Belief in Fairies

If you weren't convinced about the existence of fairies by simply explaining their origins, we will discuss our ancestors' beliefs in fairies further. In Ireland, belief in fairies was so widespread, that as recent as the early nineteen-hundreds, a man killed his wife because he thought she was stolen and then replaced by a fairy. This is part of the "changeling" legend. The Irish placed pails of cream, milk, or butter on their steps to appease the fay on certain nights of the year. Farmers left the first or last-harvested crop in the fields for the fairies to avert their tricks or hexes. Some of these traditions survive today.

The Scottish Brownie and Others

In Scotland, the belief in a house-fairy known as the brownie is still prominent. Brownies were small, stout creatures that lived in the home and helped with chores while everyone was asleep. They were helpful, benevolent fairies with a close connection to the rooster. Some say brownies could shapeshift into the form of the rooster. He would crow at dawn to announce his work was done. OR the rooster crowed to alert the brownie it was time for him to go to sleep and the people of the house to wake up. Other fairy creatures in Scotland and England include selkies, spriggans, pixies, Jenny Greenteeth, kelpies, dryads, and more.

REAL Physical Evidence of Fairies?

To truly answer the question "are fairies real", we need physical evidence. This is how science proves theories. Recently, the Smithsonian Magazine released an article about a small, human-like skeleton discovered in Chile. People said it was an alien's skeleton, others said it was a hoax. The scientists who examined DNA of the tiny skeleton decided it was a human child with genetic disorders and deformities. But no one proposed the theory of the tiny humanoid creature being a fairy. If we ever needed physical proof of fairies' existence, the proof is in this skeleton. The skeleton is too small to be human, even with extreme genetic disorders and deformities (in my opinion).

The Broighter Gold Boat

The Broighter Gold Boat was an archaeological discovery made in Ireland in the eighteen-hundreds. This tiny gold boat measures approximately seven by four inches. The detail of the boat is incredible, down to its miniature oars. Yes, this could have been a votive offering to the Celtic gods in ancient times, as theorized by scholars. I believe it's a vessel that carried fairies over water. The size is perfect and fits perfectly into our tales of the fay. What do you think? Have you seen a fairy?

The Fairy Shoe Found on Beara Peninsula

Another intriguing account of potential fairy evidence is the fairy shoe of Beara Peninsula. According to the Celtic Nations Magazine, a tiny shoe was found on a "sheep track" by a farmer who'd decided to take a short cut home that day. I'd like to mention that the shoe was found on a path used by sheep and farmers, and whether this sheep track could be a ley line or fairy path? Something to consider, for sure.

The tiny shoe was less than 3 inches in length and was found just lying on the ground. It seemed to be made in a style that was at least a century old and didn't fit any doll. Apparently, a man who ended up with the tiny shoe brought it to the U.S. and had it examined at Harvard University. Scholars there concluded the shoe was made of mouse leather and that it had eyelets for tiny shoelaces to fit through. Even more fascinating, the shoe itself showed significant wear on the heels. As if someone had walked in the shoe daily for some miles. If it was a doll's shoe or a toy, how would it have shown specific wear and tear in this manner?

If you look closely at the mythology and folklore of cultures all around the world, you will find dozens of stories. From Asia to Europe, Africa to the Americas, the belief in fairies was present for centuries. How can every culture have a belief

18

in fairies, even when these people sometimes had little to no contact with one another?

Types of Fairies Worldwide

Nothing has fascinated me more than the faery realm. As a little girl, I watched any and every movie that featured fairies, devoured fairy tale books, and had figurines all over my bedroom. It wasn't until I was a teenager that I learned there were more than a few types of fairies. And that the realm of the fay was much more beautifully complicated and dangerous than I ever imagined! The fairies we see in mainstream media are typically the garden-fairy variety or pixies. But that leaves out the brownies, elves, gnomes, dwarves, and many more.

First, What Are Fairies?

What are fairies? And where do they come from? Depending on who you ask, you'll get a different answer every time. These illusive creatures are theorized to be everything from a tiny ancient race of human beings to gods to the souls of unbaptized children. I always felt the answer was somewhere in between and maybe a mixture of a few things: they are spirits of nature, guardians of wildlife and sacred natural places, but also may once have been considered gods. And, as mentioned before, it also depends on the culture.

Different Types of Fairies All Over the World

1. Alven

Alven are a type of fairy from Holland who are attached to bodies of water: lakes, rivers, and ponds. Though the River Elbe is particularly sacred to them. Alven travel by way of bubbles – they get inside bubbles and float along to their destination. When seen, alven are tiny enough to fit in a bubble OR sometimes take the shapeshifted form of an otter. This is why their other name is ottermaaner. They come out in hordes on the full moon, dancing and playing in the moonlight reflected on the water. The Alven aren't typically mean to human beings, unless you desecrate their home or pick night-blooming flowers near their sacred river.

2. Boggarts

The Scottish boggart may be the original "boogieman" or "bogey man". They look like the Scottish brownie, but they aren't nice. And they won't do your chores. Some people believe brownies turn into boggarts when angered. A boggart is not a good fairy to have in your house, as they seek to destroy your home. Legend says they chew on the wood like a termite and will try to suffocate children at night. Enter the story of the boogey-man coming out at night and tormenting children. If they're not in a house, they're scaring travelers on rural roads.

3. Bean-sidhe, a.k.a. Banshee (Type of Death Fairy)

The bean-sidhe (banshee) is probably the most well-known death fairy from Irish lore. She is also known as the Washer at the Fords and the Wailing Woman. The Morrigan, who is a Celtic war goddess, is often associated with the banshee. And some believe they are one-in-the-same. This type of fairy is believed to be attached to the old noble Irish families. Her scream is heard right before someone dies, sometimes right outside the dying's window. If you see her washing bloody shrouds in the river, it's also a sign you or your family member will soon depart. Her presence is an omen of imminent death and therefore many people fear this type of fairy.

4. Bean-tighe: Irish House Fairy

The bean-tighe (bantee) is the Irish version of the Scottish brownie. She is a pleasant type of fairy that lives in a family's household and helps with their chores. The main difference between the bean-tighe and the brownie gender: the bean-tighe is female. The name bean-tighe translates to "woman of the house". When the bean-tighe is spotted, she's typically wearing tattered house-clothes. Her face is wrinkly and she stands no taller than a few feet. Not only does she help with household chores, but she also watches over children and animals in the house.

5. Brownies: A Type of Scottish House Fairy

The Scottish brownie isn't a dessert. He's a house fairy that lives in old manors and homes in Scotland. He is a small fairy standing about two feet tall and helps with household chores once the lady of the house goes to sleep. The brownie only aids those who are worthy, he doesn't like laziness. Never give a brownie clothes, or he might leave. Brownies might have traveled with Scottish immigrants to the United States and Canada. And he's a shapeshifter, often taking the form of the rooster to crow in the morning.

6. *Hobgoblin*

The hobgoblin is a type of fairy from Northern England and may be the same creature as the Scottish boggart. The name hobgoblin comes from hob which means elf and goblin which means mischievous fairy. According to old folklore, the hob was once a hearth spirit and helpful to the household. But as Christianity rose to power, the hob became the hobgoblin and was demonized. Hobgoblins look like Scottish brownies – small, hairy little men. They enjoyed doing chores around the house like ironing, sweeping, etc. in exchange for food offerings and libations. Shakespeare's version of Puck in Midsummer Night's Dream is probably the most famous literary hobgoblin next to Dobby of the Harry Potter Series. It seems this type of fairy is helpful until it's angered…just like it's Scottish counterpart.

7. *Buttery Sprites*

Sounds delicious, right? Unfortunately, buttery sprites are not a new flavor of soda. They're a type of fairy from England who was particularly precocious in Medieval Times. They're called buttery sprites because they are spirits who love to steal freshly churned butter! No one claims to have ever seen a buttery sprite – they come out at night and are likely invisible unless want to be seen. I picture them somewhere close to the pixie. Sprites love to irritate and play pranks on hypocritical people.

8. *Pixies*

Pixies are the most well-known type of fairy and seem to be the image most people call up when hearing the word "fairy". Other names for pixies include dusters, piskies, grigs, pechts, and pickers. They are of Scottish and English origin. Tinkerbell, the fairy in Peter Pan, is a pixie and depicts the classic piskie looks small, winged creature with a large head and tiny body. There are theories that suggest "pixie" relates to the Picts, ancient people who once occupied Scotland. Pixies love gardens full of flowers and are active on the Spring and Summer sabbats: Ostara, Beltane, Litha, and Lughnasadh. They are generally helpful but incredibly mischievous.

9. Gnomes

Gnomes are a small type of fairy that live in the roots and trunks of ancient trees. The male gnomes have long white beards and white hair. Gnomes wear red hats and the females are sometimes seen holding their tiny babies. They protect the forest and the wildlife around them, and as such are part of the traditional "elementals" in ceremonial magick. Gnomes are called upon when summoning the Guardians of the Watchtowers of the North in a magic circle. Ghob is the king of the gnome kingdom. When gnomes live in your garden, your garden will surely be blessed.

10. Elves

In Norse mythology, elves are god-like. Freyr, King of the Elves, is illustrated and treated as a god and divine ancestor to those of Swedish blood. There are light elves and dark elves in Prose Edda. While ingrained in Norse and Germanic mythos, elves are seen worldwide. They can appear as tall, radiant beings or tiny as a mouse. In Germany, elves are known as expert weavers and spinners, hence the fairy tale Rumpelstiltskin (an elf that spins gold). Elves typically travel in groups, and when they do so are called trooping elves. In the United States, elves are seen at the edges of forests and sometimes in quiet graveyards and always wear green with green hats.

11. *Callicantzaroi*

Callicantzaroi are malevolent goblin-type fairies in old Mediterranean and Anatolian folklore. Though their malevolence is debated and their reputation may have been ruined with the rise of the church. These goblins ride on the backs of chickens and their favorite food is pork. They are supposedly ugly little men who ride in groups along with other goblins and fairies. The Callicantzaroi are active on the nights approaching winter solstice and supposedly are never seen past the twelfth night. Illustrations show the callicantzaros having malformed teeth, donkey ears and goat legs. In Turkey they are equated with vampires and werewolves.

12. *Chin-chin Kobakama*

The chin chin kobakama is a Japanese house fairy that prefers the home to be kept clean. Specifically, the floors. If it's clean, they will bless the home. If it's not clean and the residents are lazy, this fairy will pick on the home's inhabitants with no regard. They look like tiny, wizened elves but are surprisingly energetic and spry. There's an old fairy tale where a woman is tormented by "little men" who live in the carpet. When her husband lashes out at them, they turn into toothpicks.

13. *Domovoi: A Type of Russian House Fairy*

The Scottish have their brownie, the Japanese the chin chin kobokama, and the Slavs have the domovoi. The domovoi are household spirits, who are fond of the hearth. They are fierce protectors of the Slavic home as long as they are fed and kept appeased. The domovoi are a type of elf and live in the hearth's flames. The domovoi is a shapeshifter and appears as a little woman, man, cat, cow, or pig depending on its mood. He is also called the Old Man of the House. This type of fairy is believed to have been an ancestor's spirit. In some tales, the eldest person would be the first to enter a new home. They would be the first to die and so become the home's domovoi. The domovoi's main job was to protect the home from other spirits, the elements, and dark magic.

14. Dryads

Dryads are originally a Greek type of tree fairy or the actual spirits of the trees. But truly their presence is worldwide. If you listen to the trees blowing in the breeze, you'll hear their whispers. Dryads appear as pure whisps of light that dart from tree-top to tree-top. Dryads may be the spirits who gave the name to the Celtic priesthood, Druids. After all, Druids' worship centered around trees and tree groves were their sanctuaries. Daphne is the most famous of dryads. In Greek mythology, Daphne was pursued by the god Apollo and thereafter turned into a laurel tree.

15. Jimaninos

The jimaninos are trooping fairies that fly in groups over Mexico particularly on holy nights of the year. When seen, they look like cupids or fat, chubby children. There are both male and female jimaninos (male = jimaninos, female = jimaninas). This is where the theory of fairies being unbaptized children's souls is perpetuated. Since the jimaninos resemble children and fly in the sky, people who see the assume they are lost children's souls.

16. Knockers

Knockers are of Cornish origin, but this type of fairy is heard all over the world. Some people don't believe they are fairies, but frightening ghosts instead. They tend to make a lot of noise, hence their name knockers. Knockers are heard deep in the earth – in caves and mines. They've scared off many miners over the centuries, some that swear they'd never return to mining. Others claim knockers lead the miners to riches. They've also been known to jump out and make funny faces at the miners. Knockers can create mine cave-ins but have also helped lost miners find their way out. Or have aided rescue teams to caved-in miners. The custom is to knock when you enter the mine to let them know you're there and doff your hat in greeting. Others feed the knockers with offerings of food.

17. Menehuna

Before the indigenous Hawaiians lived on the islands, a smaller race of people called Menehuna lived there. Some of the lakes are said to have been made by the menehuna. These fairies are tropical and are seen in the forests of Polynesia. In addition to being expert builders, they are treasure hoarders like the Irish leprechaun. They are capricious but typically benevolent to humans who respect Mother Earth.

18. Greenies

Greenies, also called moss people and flying leaves, are seen in nearly every forest in the world. They are tiny fairies that dance and flit from tree to tree. But just when you think you see them, they're gone. They are experts at camouflaging themselves, so even when you think you see them in a photo, you'll look again and nothing's there. In Germany and Switzerland, they are equated with butterflies. This winged fairy is active in Spring and Summer and are only found in the densest of woodlands. Some claim you can communicate with them by first offering fresh milk and sweets. But be careful! They are capricious like pixies and won't hesitate to play pranks or steal your things.

19. Nixen

Nixies or the nixen are water fairies with a tendency to lure unsuspecting sailors to their deaths on rocks. They also enjoy stirring up a good thunderstorm when humans are encroaching on their territory. When they leave their river homes, they are beautiful and seductive women. You may be tempted, but you'll know she's a nixie if she appears wet and covered in water plant material. This water fairy was once seen often trying to take men with them into the depths of the waters. They've been seen less frequently over the past century or so.

20. Phookas

The phooka is a fairy of Irish myth with the head of a person and the body of a horse. They are always malevolent and/or mischievous and steal crops from farmers. Especially any crops that aren't harvested before Samhain (Halloween). The phooka spooks children with no regard and have been known to kill livestock. Watch your babies, because the phooka rides around looking for the perfect child to steal and replace with a changeling. Phookas are typically seen after Samhain and before Midsummer, never in-between those times. If you want to harvest plants after sunset, you risk meeting a phooka.

21. Red Caps

As their name suggests, red caps are fairies who always wear red hats. They are solitary fairies that haunt old ruins of castles and manors in Scotland and England. Red cap sightings have been documented for centuries, even in modern times. When you see a red cap, don't get curious. Run. He is said to be a cannibal and will strike down anyone he sees that he feels is a threat. The red cap he wears is supposedly stained from blood. In addition to wearing a red cap, you'll know him by his small stature, hairy body and he carries a scythe. Perhaps he's misunderstood? But I don't think I want to find out.

22. Rusalki

This type of water fairy is of Russian origin. The rusalki appear as women bathing in rivers and lakes. They're typically not malevolent or vicious, at first, but their games can become downright frightening. You might find yourself floating face down in the river and realizing it just before taking a deep breath. Or you might find yourself lost in the woods alongside their sacred river. The rusalki are generally feared by the Slavic people because of their torturous water games. Interestingly, before the nineteenth century, the rusalki were considered benevolent especially for fertility purposes. But after they became malicious demonic mermaid type creatures. They're always seen with long green hair OR naked with long light brown hair. Some stories say they tickle men to death and climb trees in the Summer.

23. Tomtra

The tomtra is a type of Finnish house fairy that protects the household. When seen, he wears brown clothes and a green hat. He is like the Scottish brownie but a bit grumpier. If he isn't fed or angered, he will play tricks on the home's inhabitants. He particularly dislikes sloppiness, and the floors should be kept clean as much as possible. The tomtra likes throwing things, like small bouncy balls, paper clips, etc. You'll find tiny objects all over the floor when he's angry about the floor being dirty.

24. *Tuatha de Danann*

The Tuatha de Danann, or the People of the goddess Danu, were once the deities who ruled the country of Ireland. The Fomorians drove them into the hills, where they stay to this day. Technically, they are gods but were eventually said to be fairies. Some writers say they are "gods yet not gods". They are an anomole. Danu, The Dagda and The Morrigan are all gods and part of the Tuatha de Danann. They feature widely in many Irish myths and sagas and modern Celtic pagans honor them in their practice. They are trooping fairies but have every ability and opportunity to show up solitary any time any place.

25. *Leprechaun*

The leprechaun is the most famous type of fairy from Ireland. Some folks don't realize the leprechaun is of the faery realm…but he is! A capricious, gold-hoarding little man, find him with his pot of gold at the end of the rainbow. Legend says if you find him, he will grant you three wishes. The leprechaun is a solitary fairy but makes shoes for his fellow fairies. Leprechauns love gold, music, dancing, whiskey and playing pranks on humans.

26. *Monaciello: A Type of Italian House Fairy*

The monaciello is a type of Italian house fairy that guards the wine cellar. He wears a red, hooded cloak and likes to partake of the wine inventory. Provide him with regular wine offerings to keep him happy and he will continue to protect your wine cellar. Legend says the monaciello has a secret treasure, and if you can take his hood, you get his treasure. I don't recommend stealing anything from a fairy, though. It won't end well.

27. Vile

The Vile are Slavic fairies who are comparable to nymphs: long-haired, beautiful female elemental spirits. Some live in the air on clouds, some in the water, and some in woodlands. The Vile also resemble the Valkyries of Norse mythology in that they choose handsome strong men to assist in battle. They are shapeshifters and take the form of many animals including swans, wolves, and other birds. When this type of fairy is seen, they are often seen dancing in circles in the wilderness. One must never interrupt the dance of the Vile.

28. Kelpies

Kelpies are Irish water horses and a type of fairy. They are easily distinguished from physical horses because they look wet and sometimes have seaweed caught in their mane and tail. Just like with other fairies, a kelpie's demeanor varies by legend. Sometimes kelpies drag unsuspecting humans to the depths of the water, sometimes they aid humans.

29. Selkies

Selkies are shapeshifting water fairies found off the coast of Scotland, namely in Orkney. These beings are like merpeople, but different in that they have no fish fins. Instead, they take on a seal-form when in the water and shed their sealskins when on land. There are dozens of stories of men marrying selkie women only to have them unexpectedly return to their home in the sea. Crying seven tears into the sea will summon a male selkie to take as a lover, according to folklore.

30. Mermaids and Mermen

While some might not consider merpeople as a type of fairy, they are indeed supernatural beings of the elemental kind. So, we are including them here. Mermaids and mermen have been seen all over the world and nearly every culture has its own legends about them. Theories abound as to their origins: are they spirits of the ocean? Are they hybrid human beings that somehow went a different evolutionary direction? We may never know. Most merpeople appear as half-human half-fish, typically with the bottom half of their bodies covered in fish scales and ending in fins. Mermaids and mermen are known in legend to save drowning humans OR to drown humans. They may be benevolent OR malevolent, depending on the type of mermaid and its temperament.

31. Giants

Giants are yet another mythical being that we believe is part of the faery realm. Just because fairies are frequently depicted as tiny creatures with wings doesn't mean there aren't fairies of gigantic proportions. Enter the giants and ogres of fairy tale fame. Before fairy tales, giants have been ingrained in Norse religious beliefs for thousands of years (so have elves and dwarves). Giants live in their own special realm, sometimes shown as a place in the clouds (i.e. the giant in Jack and the Beanstalk).

32. Ballybogs

Ballybogs are bulbous looking little creatures that inhabit peat bogs. Some sources say they can shift into the form of frogs or other bog-dwelling animals. When they manifest in their true form, they are short and have long arms. Their noses are round and their skin is tan and/or the colors of the bog itself. This type of fairy is known to be territorial of its home, so if you decide to visit a peat bog anytime soon, consider where you're traipsing and be respectful!

Types of Mermaids Worldwide

When I was a little girl, I wanted to be part of their world. Mermaids, that is. I swam in the pool, with my feet "fused" together, and emerged to the surface only to flip my long hair behind me. Just like Ariel. I was obsessed with all things mermaids. Following this D*sney affliction (I mean, addiction), I spent years of my life researching and reading about these illusive mythical sea creatures. And I learned that there are literally dozens of types of mermaids…and they're not just seen in Europe. They're seen worldwide!

First, What Is A Mermaid, Exactly?

Are mermaids real? And what is a mermaid, exactly? These are questions that most little girls and imaginative individuals of all ages ask. There was a "documentary" some years back that gave us a glance into the supposed mermaid sightings worldwide. Unfortunately, most of the documentary was fabricated and it confused many of us. They portrayed mermaids as being real, corporeal beings with flesh and bone. I feel the problem with this depiction is that mermaids, mermen, and many other mythical sea creatures are in fact in the spirit realm. They are elementals. Guardians of sea and sky. And if they are in fact spiritual beings, this explains how they can shapeshift, traverse between worlds, and much more.

Types of Mermaids Worldwide

Mermaids are a comparative myth. This means multiple cultures, on nearly every continent, share similar legends about human-like sea creatures. Dating back thousands of years, we have archaeological proof of people's belief in these mysterious beings. There were even gods and goddesses who were portrayed as part-fish, part-dolphin, etc. This list is by no means exhaustive, but I hope you learn something new! And, for clarification, any human-like creature whose home is the sea can be called a mermaid or merman. Mer-maid means sea-maid.

1. Alven (Ottermaaner): A Type of Elven Mermaid

River Alven are an interesting type of mermaid found in The Netherlands. They are also called ottermaaner, meaning otter-men and are technically also classified as a type of elf. They are similar to the Selkie in that they shapeshift into otters using magical otter-skins (whereas the selkie shifts using seal-skin). Some say the Ottermaaner travel in bubbles, bobbing to and fro above the water. They are most seen inhabiting the River Elbe.

2. Blue Men of the Minch

The Blue Men of the Minch are the type of mermaid you don't want to meet in person. They're known for being violent and causing shipwrecks along the Scottish coastline.

They're also called Storm Kelpies. With blue skin and a craving for poetry, the Blue Men are sometimes linked to the ancient Picts of Scotland, who painted their skin blue. If you see a Blue Man, floating on top of the water, he'll ask you to recite a poem to entertain him. If you refuse, he will turn over your boat or, unbeknownst to you, lead you to your death later.

3. Camenae

Speaking of gods and goddesses, the Camenae were Greek goddesses of the sacred wells and fountains. They were invoked to guard and guide women in childbirth and eventually became syncretized with the Greek Muses. The Camenae's dedicated spring is located just outside the Porta Capena. The Baths of Caracalla sit in the valley that used to be covered in forests and springs. A site in which healing was given to those who sought it from the water goddesses. The Camenae were also known to prophesy.

4. Corrigans

The people of Brittany, France descend from the Bretons, a Celtic people who also inhabited parts of the British Isles in ancient times. And we all know the Celts had strong beliefs in faeries and elementals. Corrigans, like Camenae, are a type of mermaid that inhabit smaller bodies of water in Brittany. Rivers, springs, wells, and fountains are their home. They also share common qualities with Sirens: singing, combing their hair, and luring men to their deaths. Interestingly, they're one of few mermaids that steal children and replace them with changelings.

5. Dracs: A Dragon Type of Mermaid in France

No, we're not talking about Dracula. Though the names correlate. The syllable drac means dragon. And so, we have these French female water-serpents that shapeshift into anything they please including beautiful young women and dragons. Oddly, dracs also appear above the water as golden chalices…only to lure you to the water's edge. When you reach in to grab the treasure, the drac pulls you under! This terrifying type of mermaid is seemingly related to the dragon-spirit Melusine. They've been seen in the River Rhone but are also known to visit nearby towns searching for children and young women to steal.

6. Finfolk

The first time I read about the Finfolk, I was utterly taken. These sea gardeners are best known in the Orkeny Islands for growing and tending to lavish underwater gardens. Finfolk appear to be of the same species as your typical mermaid or merman: half-human with the tail of a fish in place of legs. Finwives (female finfolk) are beautiful, have long hair, and were often kidnapped and forced to marry human men. Finmen (male finfolk) were less attractive, had dark countenances, and cause ships to wreck when their territory is threatened. Some stories say finfolk kidnap humans and take them to their underwater world, forcing them to marry and stay there forever.

7. Mal-de-mer: An Evil Type of Mermaid

Yet another type of mermaid from Brittany is the Mal-de-mer. Their name translates to "evil of the sea" or malevolent mermaid. They are also accused of wrecking ships. Not surprisingly, mal-de-mer is also a term that means seasickness.

8. Mermaids and Mermen

The longer I study mer-beings, the more I believe mermaid and merman are more general terms for human-like sea creatures worldwide. It's a general classification. Similar to saying a blue jay is a type of bird. You'd also say a Drac or Corrigan is a type of mermaid. But, if we don't have specific names for a mermaid, this term gets the point across. As discussed, mermaids and mermen sightings have occurred all over the world for thousands of years. We have archaeological evidence of belief in mermaids dating back at least 7000 years ago on cave walls. The most recent sighting was in Kiryat Haim Beach, Israel in 2009. There was even a million-dollar reward for footage.

9. Merrows

In Ireland there are many tales of the "wee folk" (fairies), and not surprisingly, the people have their version of the mermaid/merman called merrows. Sailors and people who lived by the seashore had a whole gamut of merrow lore, and many still tell enchanting tales today. In writer W.B. Yeats' collection of Irish folk tales, there is an entire section dedicated to stories of merrows. According to legend, the merrow has a greenish tint to its skin with webbed fingers, the tail of a fish, and seaweed-green hair.

The Soul-Stealing Irish Mermaid

One particularly frightening story of the Irish mermaid tells the tale of male merrows who capture the drowned souls of sailors and trap them in pots. These pots are sunk at the bottom of the sea, never to release the poor sailors' souls…unless a willing human being were to release them. The male merrows were said to be malevolent and incredibly ugly. Perhaps this is why we have stories of female merrows seducing human men. The females would seduce young men by singing to them and then drag them under the waves to the bottom of the sea. No one knows what happened to these men, were they made into merrows themselves or did they drown?

The Merrows' Magical Red Cap

One particularly interesting aspect of these Gaelic legends is the merrows were only able to swim underwater with the aid of magic—a magical red "cap" they wore on their heads. If a person stole the merrows' cap and never returned it, the merrows would then be unable to return to their home underwater. In one legend, an Irish man uses the red cap to visit a male merrow's home under the sea.

Lost & Found: Merrows

Probably my favorite story of a real mermaid encounter is the story of an Irish man who found two dying merrows on the seashore. Apparently, they washed up to shore from a bad storm. One was badly hurt and the other was dead. The man wanted to help the merrow and took the merrow home to nurse it back to health. He kept the merrow in a tub of water and fed it shellfish and milk. The boy merrow would not drink or eat anything else offered to him. This occurred in the 1800's and was a big story in the local paper.

10. Neck or Nokk

This type of mermaid is seen in the ocean, Baltic Sea and gulfs around Scandinavian countries. The Neck or Nokk is the Norwegian version of the Nixie in Germanic lore. And just like the Nixie, she is dangerous. She seductively sings and plays beautiful harp music, luring men and then drowning them. The neck also shapeshifts.

11. Nereids

A specific kind of sea nymph who were also the daughters of Nereus and Doris. In stark contrast to the neck, nixie, and drac, nereids are helpful to humans. They are mentioned quite a bit in Greek mythology and helped Jason and the

Argonauts in their voyages. Their names include: Amatheia, Amphitrite, Asia, Calypso, Doris, Doto, Maera, Opis, Panope, Thetis, and Xantho (among many others). They've been seen with Tritons and are accompanied by dolphins and other sea creatures.

12. Ningen

Some years back, a modern Japanese legend grew to great fame worldwide. And the ningen became a cryptid that fascinated many people. The ningen is a humanoid-whale creature that reportedly was seen by Japanese fishing vessels in the Antarctic. They are described as white whales with long arms and legs, being anywhere from normal human height to 90 feet long. Some people call them "Antarctic mermaids". They're creepy if you ask me.

13. Nixen

The Nixie, plural Nixen, is a water spirit known throughout Germanic folklore. They are not to be trusted. They typically manifest as a beautiful woman, but one thing gives them away – they are always wet. Their hair drips and their skin beads up with water. Depending on the story and region, the nixie can be nice or cruel. Helpful or homicidal. In the Faroe Islands, the nixie is like the kelpie – it shifts shape into that of a horse and drowns those who try to ride it. People have used metal as a weapon against them.

15. Nommo

The Dogon tribe, located in Mali, have strong beliefs of their origins dating back thousands of years. One of those origin stories involves a mermaid-type being that came to earth from another planet long ago. These mermaid beings are the Dogons' ancestors and considered creator gods (or demi-gods). The Nommo appear on the Dogons' depictions as half-human half-fish beings. They are credited with the creation of man on this planet.

16. Roanes

Roanes are seen off the coast of Northern Ireland and are basically the same type of mermaid as the Scottish Selkie. They are shapeshifters – they take on the form of a woman or wear a seal skin to take on the form of a seal. There have been dozens of sightings over the years and hundreds of tales of Roanes (and of their cousins, the selkies).

17. Rusalki: A Type of Slavic Mermaid

The Rusalki are river mermaids in Slavic lore. They lure men, women and children to the water's edge and drown them. Legend says they'll hold you just under the surface of the water, and let you struggle, until you're no longer breathing air but water. Their skin is slippery and pale, sometimes tinted green. They have long green hair that resembles seaweed. Some scholars believe the Rusalki might have originally been goddesses in Old Rus' (Russia) that were demonized over the centuries. A mischievous and volatile rusalka is featured in Katherine Arden's Winternight Trilogy.

18. Sea Gods

It's interesting to note there are quite a few sea gods and goddesses who take the form of a mermaid or merman: half-man and half-fish. My question is what came first – the sea god or the mermaid? Some of the sea deities who manifest in mermaid/merman form include Poseidon, Triton, Neptune, the Nommo, Yemaya, Sedna, Mami Wata, Amphitrite, Glaucus and Atargatis.

19. Sirens

Sirens are a type of Greek mermaid that have been featured in many sagas, fables, and legends over the years. They make a recurrent appearance in movies and TV series in modern times. Sirens are illustrated as beautiful women with the tail of a fish OR as women who shapeshift into large seabirds. They are known to lure men to their deaths with their enchanting songs. They live on the island Sirenem scorpuli in the Mediterranean Sea.

20. *Selkies*

A lesser-known legend of a supernatural sea creature is that of the selkie. The selkie is a seal-person, or a being that can change forms between a seal and a human being, depending on if he/she is on land or sea. This legend comes from Orkney and Shetland but can be heard in tales across Ireland and Scotland, as well as in Iceland. According to legend, selkies are shapeshifters, shedding their seal-skins when they come to land.

Selkies as Wives

There are numerous stories about selkie women who are captured by sailors and taken onto land with them to be made into their loyal wives. The men were said to have hidden the selkie's seal-skin in order to keep her bound to the land. Unfortunately for these men, most of the time the selkie woman has an insatiable longing for the ocean..and if she finds her hidden seal-skin? Well, she puts it on and runs back to her home under the waves, never to be seen again.

Male Selkies

The seal-men or selkie males are said to be very attractive (as opposed to male merrows who were ugly), and legend has it that if a woman wants to have a selkie-lover she need only cry seven tears into the water and he will appear to her. Usually, these love stories are tragic and end in more tears for the human lovers. Frequently, selkies are malevolent and will seduce humans to the water and drag them under, and still other stories tell of selkies saving drowning sailors.

Origin of Selkies

There are theories of origin for selkies. One of them says that the selkies were merely women from Northern cultures that wore skins and used animal-skins on their kayaks. They came from the sea, and so therefore the legend of the seal-woman was born. Or perhaps the legend comes from old sailor stories where indeed they had sightings of seals and imagined these seals to be beautiful women instead. Today selkies are used as characters in movies, television shows, and books all over the world.

21. Shellycoats

A shellycoat is another type of English and Scottish mer-being that resides at the bottom of rivers and lakes. They wear a coat of seashells, which click and clacks when they walk on land. Some say they are dangerous, while others say they are simply mischievous. They enjoy playing pranks on nearby humans. Jacob Grimm (of the Grimm Brothers) claimed the English shellycoat is the same being as the German Schellenrock (bell coat). They've been known to make drowning sounds as a prank. And when someone comes running to help, they disappear and laugh hysterically.

22. Tritons

Triton is the father of Ariel in Disney's Little Mermaid. But his character is based on legitimate Greek mythology. Triton is a sea nymph and demi-god and is the son of the sea gods Poseidon and Amphitrite. Sometimes Tritons are a classification of sea nymphs, named for their leader. Triton holds a magical seashell, which he blows to command the seas.

23. Undines: All-Powerful Elemental

In ceremonial magical traditions, the Guardians of the Watchtowers are powerful beings that protect and wield the four elements and four cardinal directions. The Guardians of the Watchtower of the West are Undines. Undines are typically depicted as strong, powerful mermaids and mermen. This type of mermaid is also a type of elemental. They are invoked during ritual when tapping into the water element and all the water element entails. Just like the sea, Undines can be healing and destructive depending on the situation. Learn more about the Guardians of the Watchtowers.

24. Vodianoy: Another Type of Russian Mermaid

The vodioanoy is another type of water spirit in Slavic mythology. But he doesn't look quite as mystical as the Rusalka. He has the head of a frog, slimy skin, webbed hands, a fish tail and a gray beard. Interestingly, in parts of Russia, the Vodianoy is called "grandfather" and talked of as a sort of primal ancestor. When someone drowns in Russia, it's said to be the work of the Vodianoy or a Rusalka. This powerful merman also can cause storms on the water, break dams, and destroy water mills. An intriguing note – this isn't the only ancestral spirit that comes from the water. See the Nommo above. Does this idea somehow relate back to our evolution as a species? All of us emerging from the water so many millions of years ago?

25. Vodnik

See the description of the Vodianoy above to get an idea as to what the Vodnik is like. The main differences? The Vodnik is the Czech version of the Slavic Vodianoy AND the Vodnik doesn't have a frog face. Instead, his skin is green, he has gills and webbed hands. Eerily, the Vodnik are like some of the mermen in Celtic lore that keep the souls of drowned individuals in pots. How is it that two separate people had such a similar mermaid story? Perhaps these beings once existed and our ancient ancestors knew their nature intimately.

26. Kelpies

Water horse spirits are prevalent in folklore worldwide. The water kelpie is a Scottish water horse spirit. The kelpie legend is so popular, there is a large statue in Falkirk that's quite a popular tourist attraction today. The Scottish water kelpie is a spirit that inhabits bodies of water known as lochs in Scotland. The debate persists today on whether water kelpies are benevolent or malevolent creatures, as it varies by legend. The water kelpie is a large black horse shifts into human form at will (among others).

The Evil Water Kelpies

Some believe water kelpies were evil creatures, even demons, that drowned and/or ate human beings. This story was told to deter small children from going too near the water. Another legend says water kelpies shifted into good-looking young men and seduced women. Eventually dragging them into a watery grave. Even when the kelpie was in human form, it retained its horse hooves. Some say there's a connection between the kelpie and the Christian's devil because of this.

Catching & Marrying Water Kelpies

Some water kelpies were forced to stay in their human form and wed their human captors. Story goes if you keep the kelpie's silver bridle hidden away, they'll stay on land forever.

Interestingly, the silver bridle of the water kelpie is similar to the merrow's magical red cap and the selkie's sealskin. Other stories tell of capturing water kelpies using a blessed bridle. Water kelpies are sometimes thought to be dangerous, and other times helpful. If you ask me, they're ancient water spirits that guard the sacred lakes in Scotland.

Elementals and the Guardians of the Watchtowers

Before modern witchcraft, Wicca, and ceremonial magic sort of ruled the occult community. And casting a circle before ritual and invoking the elementals was a popular practice among practitioners. But what is an elemental? And are the elementals the same as the guardians of the watchtowers?

First, What is an Elemental?

First, we answer the question, what is an elemental? You've heard of the four elements, right? Earth, air, fire, and water are the four core elements according to Western magical tradition. An elemental is the spirit of an element. Just as humans have bodies AND a soul, so do elementals. The element itself (air, for example) is the physical manifestation of the elemental, while the sylph is the spirit of air. As above, so below. There are four elementals to correspond with the four elements: Gnomes are earth elementals, Undines are water elementals, Sylphs are air elementals and Salamanders are fire elementals.

Where Did the Belief in Elementals Originate?

The first wink of elemental belief originates in the Medieval Ages with alchemy. Paracelsus being one of the first alchemists to study and use the four main elements in his practice. If you ask a Wiccan today, you'll hear it's a Wiccan belief but truly we see elementals being invoked in nineteenth century ceremonial magick. Namely the Hermetic Order of the Golden Dawn. This was a Masonic-inspired secret society, if you will, of occultists who studied and practiced high magick, metaphysics, and the paranormal. The Golden Dawn's belief in elementals trickled down to more modern religions like Wicca and Aleister Crowley's Thelema. Yet the belief everything in nature has consciousness and the belief in fairies predates occult societies such as these by thousands of years.

Who Are the Guardians of the Watchtowers?

Before we go any further, let's define what the watchtowers are and how the elements and elementals may be connected. In ceremonial magick, practitioners cast a circle for protection and energy, and call on the "corners" or the four cardinal directions along with their respective elements. Typically, it goes like this: East = air, South = fire, West = water and North = earth. The corners or four cardinal directions are also known as the Watchtowers. (I literally envision a tower at each of the four directions when I call the corners.)

If you've ever watched the 90s movie The Craft, you might remember when the girls cast a circle and call the corners. "Hail to the Guardians of the Watchtowers of the East, Powers of Air and Invention, Hear Us!" Were they calling the elementals in or are the guardians of the watchtowers something completely different? My research suggests that depending on the tradition and even the individual, the Guardians of the Watchtowers can be one of many things. They could be the elementals, "kingdoms of elementals", the basic four elements, OR in some cases, archangels. Here we focus specifically on the Elementals as Guardians of the Watchtowers.

Gnomes: Guardians of the Watchtower of the North

Gnomes are the spirits of the earth element, also called earth elementals. They are guardians of the North and of the earth. The word Gnome comes from the Greek *gnoma* meaning *knowledge*. The King of the gnome kingdom, named Ghob, is sometimes invoked as a Guardian of the Watchtower of the North. Separate from being a Wiccan or ceremonial elemental, gnome folklore is found in many countries. These small faery beings live deep in ancient forests within intricate root systems. They are guardians of the ancient forests and all wildlife there. Gnomes are believed to bless one's garden and home, hence why we have gnome lawn ornaments in modern times.

Gnome elementals appear as small, wizened men and women with green and blue outfits and red caps. The men have beards. They are sometimes capricious and always protective of their natural homes. In the Order of the Golden Dawn, gnomes were considered "essential spiritual beings" invoked to praise God in a ritual called Benedicite Omnia Opera.

Sylphs: Guardians of the Watchtower of the East

Sylphs are the spirits of the air element, also called air elementals. The word sylph derives from the Greek silphe meaning butterfly. Sylphs are guardians of the East and of Air. The King of the Air kingdom's name is Paralda and is invoked as a Guardian of the Watchtower of the East. Sylphs aren't as steeped in folklore as gnomes, yet their presence is existential. I've known multiple practitioners who, after calling the corners and releasing them, have seen sylphs stick around. They seem to have a playful nature, more so than the other elementals. Sylphs appear as "tiny, winged creatures" who look "vaguely human", according to Edain McCoy. Yet modern eyewitness accounts describe them as speedy, white wisps of air.

Salamanders: Guardians of the Watchtower of the South

Salamanders are the spirits of the fire element, also known as Fire Elementals. They are the guardians of the South and

Fire. The origin of the word *salamander* isn't quite as clear but could relate to *salambe* which means fireplace. Salamanders originate in the Middle East, in the dry, hot desert where the fire element is ubiquitous. They're also said to originate in China. The King of Salamanders' name is Djinn, which links him to the Middle Eastern belief in the Djinn spirits or Djinni (where we get the Jeannie in the lamp concept).

While these beings share a name with the salamander animal, they aren't quite the same. But, in the same flame, the salamander elemental sometimes resembles a lizard. When seen, salamanders dance, slither, and flit from flame to flame in the fire. If you've taken a picture of a bonfire or candle flame and noticed faces or small, darting dragons, you've seen the salamander elementals.

Undines: Guardians of the Watchtower of the West

Undines are the spirits of the water element, also called Water Elementals. They guard the West and Water. The word *undine* comes from the word *unda* meaning wave. Undines are found everywhere there is a body of water. They often manifest in the form of a mer-being, half-human half-fish, but present themselves in any form they choose. They've also been known to look like kelpies – water horses. Their origins are Greek and Middle Eastern, and according to Edain McCoy, the undines were considered "demi-gods" by the ancient Romans. They are also called sea sprites and sea guardians. Niksa is the King of the Undines.

Why Call on the Elementals as Guardians of the Watchtowers?

You don't have to be Wiccan or a ceremonial magician to cast a circle and call the elementals. In fact, I recommend it to anyone who wants to perform an elaborate ritual on a sabbat that might need to raise extra energy or require extra protection. When you invoke the elementals and call on them as guardians of the watchtowers, you aren't just calling the elements – you're giving them a name. Giving someone or something, a name is a powerful gift.

When you call on the elementals and ask them to aid your workings, you call on the very essence of the four elements…the basis of all life on this planet. THAT is power! The elementals are known for aiding magical workings of all kinds and should be thanked and released when your circle is opened at the end of ritual. Learn how to cast a circle here if you don't know how. Then refer to the graphic above for how to call the guardians of the watchtowers.

The Irish Banshee and Leanan sidhe

She stands just outside the window with a mourning wail so shrill, the life drains from your face. But you aren't the one dying. She's here to mourn another. The beating of wings, a gasp of wind, and she's gone. And so is your family member. Is she a guide to the afterlife? Or an omen? The Irish banshee is a popular folkloric figure from the pages of history. You might have heard the term banshee before, such as in the band name Siouxsie and the Banshees or maybe in a horror movie. But the belief in the banshee isn't modern, it's ancient. Here we'll explore the origins, characteristics, and frightening aspects of the Irish banshee and introduce a vampiric fairy, the Leanan sidhe.

What or Who is the Irish Banshee?

In Celtic fairies' mythology, the Irish banshee plays an important role. Her name the banshee, or in Gaelic bean-sidhe, means "woman of the fairy mound". In Scotland, she's the cointeach. In Ireland the sidhe were the people of the hills, also called the good folk. Or in layman's terms – fairies. Fairies are depicted as small, winged, and helpful in growing gardens and saving princesses. However, the true nature of the sidhe is much different. They are unpredictable and don't follow human rules or societal values. Some of the faery folk are mischievous, while others' true intentions are never quite known. The Irish banshee being one of the latter.

What does the Banshee look like? She looks different depending on the region, which is why I believe there are multiple banshees. Sometimes she's wearing all white with long dark hair, sometimes she's dressed in green and looks like she's been sleeping in a swamp. The Banshee can be young or old, and in crone form, she typically has long gray or white hair and wears white or gray. Interestingly, in some tales, the Banshee shapeshifts into a crow, weasel, and other animals connected to witchcraft.

The Irish Banshee's Scream and Origins

The banshee is well known in Ireland and Scotland for her keening (or wailing scream), which she unleashes upon an unsuspecting family before someone in the family dies. In old Irish lore, this is typically a member of one of the old Irish families of Milesian descent. According to Ireland's Eye, the five families haunted by the Banshee are the O'Connors, the O'Neills, the O'Briens, the O'Gradys, and the Kavanaghs. When the banshee's scream is heard, it's truly terrifying. Either of the banshee herself OR of the thought of a family member's imminent death.

Another theory is the Banshee isn't a fairy but a ghost that attaches itself to a family. Which also means, this ghost could be the spirit of an ancestor. An ancestor whose job is to warn the family of the death AND mourn their descendant's death.

The Wailing Women and Goddesses

An interesting connection to note, in ancient times, wailing women (also called keeners) were women whose job it was to cry loudly, pray for, and kneel next to the dead. This was customary as a means of showing respect for the newly deceased. "In Jeremiah 9, wailing women are the ones who voice the pain and whose laments serve as memory of what and who were lost. Without the wailing women's witness, victims of violent attacks will fall into oblivion." From Calling the Keeners: The Image of the Wailing Woman As Symbol of Survival in a Traumatized World by L. Juliana M. Claasens. This was obviously an important job to ancient peoples, and one that was widespread across the globe.

Another connection is a ghost called The Wailing Woman. This legend comes from Mexican lore and tells the story of a woman who loses her children and her own life, then spends eternity looking for them from beyond the grave. She is often found haunting bodies of water and crossroads, and her more popular name is La Llorona. They call her the Wailing Woman because of the horrifying cries that come out of her mouth.

Most will say the Irish banshee is a type of fairy, because of her connection to the sidhe. However, we could argue that she might be something else, a ghost or demonized goddess perhaps. In the same breath, the sidhe, or ALL fairies, are ghosts or demonized gods and goddesses from ancient times. Fairies in Ireland are thought by some to be the Tuatha de Danann, a race of godly beings who were driven into the hills prior to the Iron Age. In fact, the goddess Cliodhna is even said to be the Queen of the Banshees".

Washer at the Fords

In Irish fairies' mythology, the banshee is sometimes seen washing bloody clothing in the river, which gained her another name – the Washer at the Fords. This is another warning of imminent death. When seen, the banshee is described as either an old hag surrounded in an eerie mist, or as the most beautiful Irish noblewoman that ever lived. Some say the Banshee is an entirely different spirit than the Washer at the Fords.

The Banshee in Scotland and Cornwall

In Scottish fairies' mythology, she sits near the door of the dying. And in Cornish lore she's seen outside the dying's window. Some say she flaps her wings against the window, and this sound has been mistaken as a crow's wings over the centuries. The fairies are known shapeshifters, so I believe the Banshee shifts into the form of a crow, connecting her to the Irish goddess of death The Morrigan.

What or Who is the Leanan sidhe?

The Leanan Sidhe is another complex folkloric figure in Irish fairy mythology. Her name translates to fairy lover, as her purpose is to take a human lover as a mate. This beautiful fairy woman lives in sacred wells and streams, but unfortunately, you can't trust her beauty. She's vampiric in nature, because she sucks the life out of her lovers directly after gifting them with unbelievable musical talent.

The Leanan sidhe's Red Cauldron

No one knows if there are multiple Leanan sidhe or if she's one spirit, like the Irish banshee. Other legends talk of the Leanan sidhe drinking her victims' blood and preserving it in a red cauldron. A cauldron that's theorized to be the source of her beauty and power. Cauldrons are associated with witches and are the source of wisdom and rebirth, indicating the Leanan sidhe was once a wise, powerful goddess (like the Welsh Celtic Cerridwen). In Irish fairy mythology, they say the only way to the only way to escape the Leanan sidhe's allure is to call out to the Irish Sea God Manann.

Kelpies: Mystical Celtic WATER Horse

A shrill neigh fills the air around you. A thick green mist envelopes you and blurs your vision of the path before you. You only had to make it down to the water and back home with a bucket full. But now it's too late. The dangerous creature your mother and grandmother warned you about is within mere feet of you. You never believed it…until now. Come with us on a (safe) journey to the water's edge, where we'll peer into the life and legend of the Kelpies, mythical Celtic water horses. We'll also hear tales of actual kelpie sightings, not only in the British Isles but worldwide.

What Are These Mystical, Illusive Kelpies, Exactly?

To put it simply, kelpies are mythical water creatures from the Celtic lands that typically manifest as white or black phantom horses near bodies of water. Some sources claim the kelpies haunt running bodies of water like rivers and streams, while others claim they also haunt lakes. There are multiple names for kelpies, depending on the country and region. In the

Orkney and Shetney Islands, they're called nuggies (I think this is my favorite name for them). You'll also hear them referred to as Uisges and Fuath in Scotland and Ireland.

The Kelpie or Shoney and the Goddess Sjofn?

In Cornwall, England the kelpie is called a shoney. Potentially echoing an old pagan goddess of the sea called Sjofn, brought to the Isles by the Norse Vikings. Sjofn is one of the goddess Frigg's handmaidens and is specifically known for her domain over affection. She watches over children and stirs up affection between two individuals, including between children and parents, people and animals, and others. She is a peacemaker and aids in relationship bonds. Her powers seem to be in direct opposition to what the kelpie's legend states. Unless, like so many other fairies and mythical creatures, the kelpie was once a benevolent creature who was demonized by the church over time.

The word kelpie is believed to translate to "heifer" or "colt", but no one knows the true origins of the word. I can't help but notice the correlation between the word Kelpie and the word kelp, referring to a brown algae seaweed that is pervasive in waters throughout the world. Interestingly, scholars aren't sure where the word kelp originates, but speculate it has something to do with the seaweed being burnt into ash in the sixteenth century for its sodium, iodine and potassium components. And have you ever noticed how the water kelpie in Fantastic Beasts is depicted…like it's literally made of kelp?

What Do Water Kelpies Look Like?

When kelpies manifest, they are typically either white or black horses with dripping wet manes and tails. Sometimes their hooves are backwards and sometimes they have a greenish glow or tint to their fur. Kelpies are almost always seen at the water's edge or very close to the water. Their temperament, at least as far as the Medieval Age onward, is malevolent and cannibalistic. Kelpies use their magic and shapeshifting abilities to lure animals, humans, and other fairies towards them. Then kidnap, drown and eat their prey in their watery homes. When they're in human form, they wear green clothing and their wet hair typically gives them away. Sometimes you'll even see seaweed stuck in their hair. Or wet footprints behind them.

What Do Kelpies Do?

It's generally known that kelpies are solitary creatures, haunting lakes, rivers, and streams alone. But they tend to exert the same qualities. This is what we know that kelpies do:

- manifest as horses near bodies of water
- shapeshift into attractive young men or women
- act docile to lure in their prey
- kidnap humans, animals and other fairies
- drown and eat their prey
- sometimes sing or talk to lure in their victims
- sometimes capture humans and take them as their husbands/wives
- kidnap young women as midwives and wetnurses
- summon floods to use in capturing prey

Is the Kelpie a Type of Elemental or Fairy?

Most people are inclined to believe the kelpie is a type of fairy or elemental. A guardian of ancient waterways, particularly in the British Isles and Ireland. However, it's interesting to note water horses and creatures like the kelpie are found all over Europe and were even reportedly seen in the New World (settlers in Maryland claimed there were kelpies in the Chesapeake Bay and its tributaries).

Their shapeshifting abilities point towards their affinity with the fairy folk. All mythical water creatures have this ability – to change form from horse or other creature into a beautiful young maiden or strapping young man. With a mission of luring their prey ever closer – sometimes to eat them, sometimes to marry them and take them to the Otherworld. When we think of the kelpie in a human-shifted form, we see clear resemblance to the Germanic nixie and the Faroese nykur. The Nykur particularly, as it's a water entity that typically appears as a white horse. All these beings are referred to as "water sprites" by folklorists and so we can also apply this train of thought to the Celtic water kelpies.

"From haunted spring and grassy ring

Troop goblin, elf and fairy,

And the kelpie must flit from the black bog-pit,

And the brownie must not tarry."

~ The Fairy Faith in Celtic Countries by WY Evans-Wentz

OR Are Kelpies Actually Guides to the Afterlife?

As I was researching, I had a big epiphany. Since the ancient Celts believed the Otherworld (afterlife) and land of the fae was located under the sea, it's not far-fetched to think the kelpie was originally a psychopomp. A psychopomp being a spiritual guide that leads souls to the other side upon death. Horses, especially white horses, are intricately woven into Celtic mythology and lore. They're considered otherworldly creatures and appear in the mythos time and time again accompanying a hero or god or being the embodiment of a goddess.

Ancient Horse Cults and Deities

According to blogger Eric W. Edwards, there were prevalent horse cults stretching across the ancient world including in Europe with the Greeks, Celts, Germanic, and Slavic tribes. As well as in India and Mongolia. Horses were sacred animals with divine powers. And they were often linked to deities who ruled over polar domains like life and death, day and night, the sun and moon.

In ancient Ireland, Macha was a horse goddess who presided over the sun, fertility, motherhood but also over war and death. To the ancient Slavs, their gods Chernobog and Belobog were the personification of night and day, as well as life and death. And they were frequently depicted as riding a black horse and a white horse, respectively. The goddess Rhiannon, a fairy princess from the Welsh Otherworld, rides a white horse in the Mabinogion. The Norse psychopomps called Valkyries ride horses made of white clouds.

It's even said that Poseidon was originally a white horse emerging from the ocean waves. Even if he wasn't a water horse himself, he fathered two divine horses: Pegasus and Arion. Sailors were known to drown horses as sacrifice to Poseidon before long journeys across the sea. This was to appease the powerful sea god. Some even believe water kelpies might be the ghosts of these sacrificed horses from ancient times. There's evidence that horses were sacrificed all over Europe including in Northern Denmark in an ancient bog. The Valmose bodies were found preserved in a bog along with horses and oxen.

Demonized Guides to the Afterlife

Water kelpies are typically seen as one of two colors: black or white. So, the question is – are water kelpies a misunderstood and misconstrued remnant of ancient horse cults and deities? The fact that most legends tell of kelpies dragging people underwater to their deaths points to an earlier belief in otherworldly guides who symbolically protected souls on their way to the afterlife. Perhaps twisting and demonizing the mythos of ancient horse gods into human-devouring kelpies made it easier for the church to convert pagans.

The Kelpie of Loch Ness

I'm sure you've heard of Loch Ness (Lake Ness) in Scotland before. But you've likely heard of it because of an ages-old legend of a cryptid named Nessie, a.k.a. the Loch Ness Monster. Fascinatingly, the famous lake has also been the haunt of a water kelpie in older times. This is a story I discovered in a book called Scottish Folk and Fairy Tales by Theresa Breslin.

Once a father, mother, and son lived near Loch Ness. The winter had been harsh, the father found himself weak, and they had no livestock. One night, the man spotted a large horse grazing near Loch Ness. And he decided to try to mount the horse and bring it home to aid in plowing the fields. His wife warned against it, saying the horse was no horse but a water kelpie. And that no man could tame a kelpie with a plain rope.

The man ignored his wife's desperate pleas and mounted the kelpie. The water horse grew two times in size, sparks shot out from under its gigantic hooves, and it suddenly breathed fire. Its mane turned into green snakes and grasped the man's hands firmly. Sadly, the man tried to fight his way off when the kelpie took off towards the water, but to no avail.

The mother and the boy grew hungrier and weaker by the day. Three times the boy meets a spaewife (a wise woman) who gives him three magical items and three pertinent pieces of advice. When he attempts to catch the kelpie, he is successful using the spaewife's charms: a shawl to use as a saddle over the kelpie's back, salt that killed the serpents on the kelpie's mane, and an iron horse's bridle.

The MacGregor Clan's Kelpie Bridle

The MacGregor Clan claims to have (or had) a kelpie's bridle in their possession for at least a century or two. I particularly love this story because I descend from a branch of MacGregors. Anyway, a MacGregor ancestor named James learned that if he could steal a kelpie's bridle away, he'd have possession of great magical powers. For a kelpie's power lies in its bridle, like how a red cap's shapeshifting and magical powers were in his red cap. So, one day, he approached a kelpie near Loch Ness, jumped towards it, cut its bridle, and took off running.

Apparently, as soon as the magical bridle had been pulled off the kelpie's neck, the kelpie shrank into the form of an old man. A very angry old man who chased James all the way home, trying to either coax or frighten him into returning his bridle. James refused and for many years the MacGregors claimed to still have the kelpie's bridle in their possession (along with a magical mermaid stone!)

How to Defeat Or Catch Kelpies

If you've ever seen a kelpie, you're fortunate (or not so fortunate) because they've supposedly not been seen for many years. Let's say you're being tormented by a kelpie who haunts the pond in your backyard or the creek on your property. According to lore, here's how you catch and/or defeat a bothersome kelpie:

- Similar to werewolves, a silver bullet will defeat a kelpie
- An iron spear will also kill a kelpie
- If you can steal a kelpie's bridle, you will have power over it and magical powers
- Salt will ward off a kelpie and prevent its mane from turning into snakes
- Separating your hand from its mane will allow you to dismount the kelpie (some use salt, one little boy actually cut off his finger to escape!)
- A bridle made of iron slipped over a kelpie's head will give you control over the water horse
- If you want to ride a kelpie, put something between you and its skin, else you'll get stuck and the kelpie will kidnap or drown you
- Wear a bag of salt around your neck if going near a kelpie's watery home
- Keep a piece if iron on you near mysterious bodies of water or known kelpie haunts

The BEST Way to Stay Safe Near A Kelpie's Home

Here's my advice when it comes to the mystical, dangerous kelpie – just stay away from them. If you see a lone horse, wandering near a body of water by itself, it might be best to leave it be. PARTICULARLY if the horse has a wet tail or mane, a green tint to it, reversed hooves or a wild look in its eye. Unless you have an iron bridle with you, search for a potential owner but don't approach it. I believe even though these creatures may be benevolent, there's too many legends that tell of their cannibalistic ways. So, it's best to leave them be.

Fairies in America: Fairy Lore and Sightings

The belief in fairies is a worldwide phenomenon. Enchanting stories of green elves, pixies, trolls, and sprites abound in countries like Ireland and Germany. We don't hear many stories of Native American fairies or different types of fairies in America. But remember – fairies are everywhere! Because fairies are nature spirits, they're typically seen in undisturbed, natural places. The Native Americans tell stories of encounters with the little people – how they helped children or taught shamans. The fairies in America can be territorial depending on the type. Come with me on a journey to find fairies in America.

Fairies in America: Green Elves & Pixies

Elves come from Scandinavian and Celtic mythology. According to Prose Edda, there are two types of elves – light and dark. In America, elves are earthly beings who are dressed in green. In A Witch's Guide to Faery Folk, Edain McCoy refers to this kind as green elves. Green elves have green-tinted skin and sometimes wear green caps on their heads. The green elves in America are shorter in height and are encountered on the edges of forests and in graveyards. They're like elves in Irish folklore. These beings live in the trees and so protect their home and surrounding wildlife. In Ireland, they are seen near ancient burial mounds, which could indicate their connection with the dead or confirm that "fairyland" is somewhere underground.

When I lived in Maryland in my teens, we had large trees on our property. One tree always felt incredibly magical to me. One day we had a psychic visit the house and mentioned the "tiny, winged fairies" flitting around this oak tree. My mom and I agreed that it was indeed a fairy tree. Because of this experience and other experiences with a grapefruit tree in my Florida backyard, I believe there are small, winged fairies like pixies in America as well as in Europe (and maybe worldwide!)

Household Fairies in America

It is possible that certain fairies traveled to America with our ancestors. The Brownie, a Scottish house fairy, is thought to have been brought to Canada and the U.S. with Scottish immigrants beginning in the seventeenth century. Tales are told online from various Americans of signs of brownies living in older Colonial homes. It's not often they're discovered living in a modern or newly constructed house – they like to stick to one family and most are attached to the first Scottish immigrant families that settled here. However, some Scottish American people claim to have attracted them into their homes using offerings and other tactics.

The Tomtra: Finnish House Fairy

The Tomtra is a house fairy that's been brought to America by Finnish immigrants. Like the Brownie's attachment to Scottish immigrant families, the tomtra is attached to the Finnish immigrants. If you are Finnish American or have Finnish blood, the tomtra may take up residence in your home. The difference between the tomtra and brownie is the tomtra is a bit more mischievous. He will protect your home from invaders, spiritual and physical, but he will also play tricks when he is bored or irritated. One American woman claims she's had small objects like jewelry and pebbles thrown at her while in her bedroom.

Native North American Beliefs in Fairies

Menehune: Native Hawaiian Fairies

The Native Hawaiians have their own legends of little people called the Menehune. The Menehune were a small indigenous people who lived in Hawaii before the Tahitian people came to reside there. Hawaiian legend tells of these little people building some of the islands' sacred places such as certain ponds and mounds. They were thought to live deep in the forests and valleys. Compare the Menehune to the Native American legends of little people – there are striking similarities. The Menehune were between six inches and two feet tall, according to legend, and despite their small stature were able to build entire structures overnight.

Scholars believe the Menehune were the first people of Hawaii, present before the Tahitians, and were driven into the forests during the Tahitian invasion in 1100 AD. Were the Menehune small in stature or were they small in the eyes of the Tahitians? Some claim to see the Menehune, but often the sightings are discredited because they are children. In my opinion, children see fairies in America easier than adults because their minds are still fresh and open.

Little People in Nova Scotia

The Eskasoni tribe in Canada tell stories about the "little people." There's a hill in Nova Scotia where the Eskasoni claim the little people have lived for centuries. The townsfolk warn their children against going to the mountain, for fear the little people will take them away. Remarkable stories of the Eskasoni people encountering the "little people" or fairies are detailed in the documentary The Fairy Faith.

Choctaw Beliefs in Fairies

The Choctaw tribe believed in the little people and called them the Kwanokasha. The Kwanokasha were known to capture young men and take them on a quest. Three wisemen would wait at a cave opening for the Kwanokasha and the Choctaw boy and present the boy with three things: a knife, a bag of poisonous herbs, and a bag of healing herbs. If the boy chooses the knife, he was destined to be a killer. If he chooses the bag of poisonous herbs, he will provide bad medicine to his people. But, if he chooses the bag of good healing herbs, he would be a powerful medicine man. Just like the Hawaiians and the Shoshone, the Choctaw believed the little people lived in caves.

Shoshone and Cherokee Fairy Legends

Just as the Scottish and English have their fairy folklore, the Native Americans have theirs. The Shoshone tribe believed in a race of tiny people they called the Nimerigar. These tiny people lived in the Rocky Mountains and were aggressive to outsiders. If anyone came near their territory, they'd shoot poisoned-tip arrows at them. The San Pedro Mountain mummy called into question the legitimacy of the Shoshone's fairy legends. This mummy was a small being discovered in the mountains in 1932. The mummy's body disappeared in the 1950's, so we might never know if it was a real fairy body or not.

The Cherokee once believed in three kinds of little people: the rock people, the laurel people, and the dogwood people. They each had their own temperaments and each taught the Cherokees different lessons. The rock people hurled rocks at anyone who got close, like the nimerigar of Shoshone legend. They were territorial and aggressive. The laurel people were mischievous and played tricks on people for fun compared to many of the European fairy legends. The dogwood people were good-natured and known to help heal. There have been fairies in America for just as long as they've been in Europe.

The Crow Tribe's Fairy Beliefs

The Crow believed in little people called the Nirumbee. The Nirumbee lived in the Pryor Mountains and gave visions to Plenty Coups an early twentieth century Crow chief. According to legend, the fairy-vision given to Plenty Coups kept the Crow people safe and united. The Crow people say when they pass Pryor Gap they leave offerings to the little people.

Real Encounters with Fairies in America

Fairies in America don't just live in legend and lore, they've shown themselves to lucky individuals. In the late 1800's, an entire group of people saw fairies flying above Chimney Rock in North Carolina. It was documented by the nearest town's scholars.

A Professor is Called

In 1891, a professor was working in his North Carolina home when there was a knock at the door. A few children stood there and pleaded with the professor to come to the side of Chimney Rock. There were "people floating around on the side of the mountain", the children claimed. The professor dismissed their story as a prank and sent them away. But then, a few minutes later, another knock. This time it wasn't the mischievous children but an elderly woman from town. She also pleaded with him to come and see the "ghosties" on the side of Chimney Rock. At this point he decided he'd accompany the old woman to Chimney Rock to assure her there was no supernatural thing floating around on the side of the mountain.

A Real Fairy Sighting at Chimney Rock

The professor accompanied the woman to Chimney Rock and, to his amazement, saw what they had seen. There were dozens of bright beings flying around the side of the mountain…right there on the side of the mountain! He couldn't believe what he was seeing. Was this real? These beings were bright and wearing white gowns, they looked like humans but were flying. There were dozens of these fairies, even appeared to be men, women, and children. More townspeople went that day to see the real fairies or little people, some in later years claiming they were angels, and the story lived on for years afterwards at Chimney Rock.

Strange Fairy Music

A mother and her children decided to have a picnic in the forest. While eating lunch, the family heard strange music playing close-by. It sounded unlike any music they'd ever heard and they found it particularly strange because there were no houses in the woods, nor had they seen any people nearby. The music got louder and began coming closer. The mother didn't want to stick around to see what was making the music, so she gathered her children and left. The little girl, who is now a woman, didn't just hear music that day – she saw small people dancing in a circle in the woods. She didn't tell people for many years for fear they wouldn't believe her.

Tiny Fairies on the Shelf

A little girl and her sister awoke one morning to see a tiny group of fairies dancing on their toy shelf. They were tiny, winged people and seemed to be friendly and happy. She woke up early every morning to try to see the fairies again, but neither her nor her sister ever saw them again. To this day, the woman swears fairies exist.

The Little Person Mummy

There is a mystery surrounding a "little mummy" discovered in the 1930's in the San Pedro Mountains. Because the little mummy was discovered in a cave, people though there was once a tiny race of cave-dwelling humans there. The little mummy was sitting upright and had a flat skull. It had tan skin and sat about 7" tall, so if it stood up it might have been a foot tall. Could the little mummy have been proof of the "little people" or fairies described by Native Americans? Unfortunately, the little mummy disappeared in the 1950's, so no further testing has been done. Scientists have studied the photographs and claim it's the mummy of an anencephalic fetus. But why did the little mummy have a full set of adult teeth?

More Fairy Sightings

An American woman claims she's seen numerous fairies during paranormal investigations including a green elf in a cemetery, a sylph (air fairy) that flies by her house, and even has photographic evidence of the existence of the Green Man in America. Real encounters with fairies in America have been happening for hundreds of years and still happen today.

Because of my articles on fairies, I receive emails from people who have pictures of fairies in the forests of America. Whether fairies are real, physical beings or spiritual beings, I cannot decide. But I know they exist in one form or another and they are prevalent in America.

Fairy Changelings: Taken by the Fairies

In today's world, fairies are depicted as cute, sparkly beings with paper thin wings. The online new age community spreads the misconception that fairies are "beings of divine light" and healers. In their defense, the idea of fairies from our childhood fairy tales indeed delights us and entices us to reminisce. But this fluffy image of the fairy isn't historically accurate. In fact, our European ancestors feared most of the fairy people. The fairy changeling, and the process of adopting one, was perhaps the most feared type of fairy, which we will discuss in detail here.

Our European Ancestors' Belief in Fairies

The Irish people believed (and still believe) strongly in fairies. They are called different things in Ireland and Scotland, depending on the region and person. Some terms you'll hear include the "good folk" the "wee folk" or the "sidhe". The term "good folk" can give the wrong impression. It doesn't mean the fairies were always benevolent in nature. Instead, the Irish figured the name "good folk" would at least appease the fairies. Not draw them to anger. The fairy folk were acknowledged and frequently feared. This is why there are stories of leaving offerings to the fairies on doorsteps, hanging horseshoes over barn doors, and never traveling during twilight hours. These were a means of appeasing and avoiding the good folk. Staying out of their way and in their good favor.

Dangerous Fairy Raids

Legends tell of unlucky individuals who run into the fairies while they are out on one of their "raids" (rides) through the countryside. Sometimes the experience is positive, but often the individual is abducted. Then taken on a ride through the countryside OR straight to fairyland. Once a person returns from fairyland, they are forever changed…years have gone by and they find themselves in an old, frail body and all their loved ones gone.

When Led to One's Death…

The Will O' the Wisp was a fuzzy, blue, or white light that led twilight or late-night travelers astray. Sometimes it even led them over a cliff and to their deaths. I could go on and on with stories of how the "good folk" weren't always so good to humankind. And from these beliefs emerged the fairy changeling.

What is a Fairy Changeling?

What is a fairy changeling and why were they so feared? A fairy changeling was a fairy child left in place of a kidnapped human child. Remember, science and modern medicine weren't advanced then. So, our European ancestors believed when things went wrong, when crops failed, when cows didn't give milk, it was because of the fairies. (When they weren't blaming the faires, it was most definitely the local witch's fault). When a baby was born with defects, or if it grew sick, they believed it was a fairy changeling and that the real human baby had been whisked away by the fairies.

You might think, I'm sure a fairy baby is a beautiful being so would people really mind? I'm being somewhat sarcastic here, it's just a joke folks. But seriously, fairy changelings were the opposite of pretty or cute. The folklore tells many stories of the baby being kidnapped and a hideous, deformed creature being left in its crib. Only to scare the living daylights out of the child's poor parents the next morning.

Why Were Humans Replaced with Fairy Changelings?

But why would fairies steal human children and leave their own? Some said fairies envied human children because of their beauty. While others said fairies stole human children to raise as their own and then use in their evil doings later on. Still others believed the fairies replaced human children with fairy changelings so that their babies would be fed and cared for by rich human beings. Then they would return to take the fairy changeling once it had grown big and strong. But the fairies didn't just steal babies, they were known to abduct adults…people they felt had a particular skill they could use. People they thought might be magical in nature.

Who Was At Risk of Being Replaced?

People who were most at risk for being kidnapped and replaced by fairy changelings included newlywed brides and newborns (along with new mothers). The thought was that brand new babies who weren't purified or baptized were at high risk of being fairy napped. As were their mothers or anyone else who wasn't baptized. New brides were at risk because they were in a "pure" state, before consummating their marriage with their husbands.

Safeguarding Babies and Mothers from the Fairies

According to W.Y. Evans-Wentz, "many precautions were taken to safeguard them until purification and baptism took place, when the fairy power became ineffective." These precautions included placing iron around the bed, burning leather in the room, and feeding the mother and baby a special cow's milk. This milk was infused with a plant called pearlwort, which was a plant thought to ward off the fay.

Smoke Cleansing to Ward Fairies. Secret Names.

And according to Edain McCoy, fairy changelings were avoided by using smoke in an area to ward off the fairies. As smoke was known to be a common fairy deterrent. In addition, families would keep their children's true names secret and call them a nickname or by their middle name instead. This is why there were so many Marys and Johns, etc. running around in those days! If the fairies didn't know your real name, they had no power of you. Names had power.

Horrifying Ways to Get Rid of Changelings

If you suspected your loved one was taken and a fairy changeling left in their place, there were ways to tell. Many stories tell of parents putting the fairy changeling into the fireplace, only to watch the fairy changeling shoot up the chimney and leave for good. The next day, or by that night, the human child was brought home. But these are TALES, remember. Unfortunately, people believed this was a real thing even a century ago! That sounds like a long time ago, but truly a hundred years is a small span of time. Your great grandparents might have been alive then!

The Sad Story of Bridget Cleary, the "Fairy Changeling"

In Ireland in 1895, a woman named Bridget Cleary came down with bronchitis. She had been ill for days and was even visited by the local doctor who confirmed the illness as bronchitis. Bridget's husband decided the medicine he was supposed to give his wife wouldn't work. That, in fact, his wife was a fairy changeling in disguise. That his real wife had been "taken by the fairies" and replaced with this coughing, weakened fairy changeling. There were a few events that led Michael Cleary to this conclusion. One, that his wife was wearing the devil's colors, and two that she was receiving a lot of attention around town for her personality and tailoring skills. It sounds to me like Michael was feeling insecure and less of a man and so his paranoid mind and superstition took over all logic. To get his wife back, he carried out some of the worst superstitions about fairy changelings.

Michael Cleary's Trial: The Fairy Changeling Murder Case

Michael Cleary was charged with murder just days after Bridget's burnt body was found buried in a ditch. Bridget had urine thrown on her and was burnt in the fireplace by Michael Cleary and other members of her family. Why was she tortured in such a hideous manner? They ALL believed she was indeed a fairy changeling, and to get their beloved Bridget back, they had to perform these tasks to expel the fairy imposter. Bridget never came back, because she was a sick woman who needed medicine and her family's love. This story always makes me so sad! It was even featured in an episode of "Lore" on Amazon Prime just last year. A popular Irish nursey rhyme goes, "Are you a witch? Are you a fairy? Or are you the wife of Michael Cleary?"

Household Fairies & Elves

Before Alexa and Google Home devices to remind us of when to complete our errands and chores, there were lucky people who had house fairies who helped with chores around the house. The house elf finished the woman of the house's leftover cleaning, cooking, and mending. Wouldn't that be nice to have a fairy in your home helping you finish your chores while you sleep?

Depending on the region, there are different types of house elves and house fairies and different names for each. The Scottish have the Brownie, which is the most well-known of the house elves. There's the Clurichaun and Beantighe in Ireland, and the Moniacello in Italy. Some are beneficial to have in your home, while others might wreak havoc should you make them angry.

1. The Scottish Brownie

The most well-known and loved house elf in folklore is the Scottish Brownie. The Brownie is a small male creature, between one and two feet tall, who takes up residence in a deserving family's home. The Brownie resides in Scotland, but some say the Scottish immigrants brought the Brownie with them to the United States and Canada in the seventeen and eighteen hundreds. The Brownie's temperament is mild, and he is rather helpful with chores around the house.

When the woman of the house goes to bed, he finishes her chores. The Brownie is helpful on the farm. He brings in food and firewood and is a shapeshifter who shifts into the form of a rooster to crow in the morning. Others believe the rooster is a friend of the Brownie's and crows to tell him when to go to bed (although humans believe the rooster crows to wake us up in the morning). The Mother Goose Rhyme "I Had a Little Rooster" demonstrates the belief in the Brownie taking on the form of the Rooster.

How to Attract a Brownie

The Brownie enjoys a family who is kind and hard-working, and typically takes up residence in a warm nook or cranny like an undisturbed cupboard or high shelf. Attract them to your home with offerings of bread, honey, sweet cream, cakes and ale. Folklore says to never give clothing to a Brownie (or any house elf) as they will take the gift and leave. JK Rowling uses this bit of lore in her famous novel series. Harry Potter gives Dobie a sock, thereby granting Dobie his freedom from servitude to the Malfoy family. It is very good luck to have a Brownie living in your house, not just for the fact that they help with chores, but also because they keep bad spirits away and bring abundance to the family.

> CANTO IV.
>
> His Nourture.
>
> "Oh, when I was a little Ghost,
> A merry time had we!
> Each seated on his favourite post,
> We chumped and chawed the buttered toast
> They gave us for our tea."
>
> "That story is in print!" I cried.
> "Don't say it's not, because

2. The Bean-Tighe: The "Irish Brownie"

Like the Scottish Brownie, the Irish Bean-tighe (pronounced ban-tee) is one of the benevolent Irish house fairies that looks after a nice family. The main difference between the Brownie and the Bean-tighe is gender. The Bean-tighe is a small elderly female creature who wears tattered old-fashioned dresses and has a wrinkled face. Her name translates to "woman of the house", and her name sounds like the Beansidhe (banshee). Both creatures are linked to the old Irish families. But in opposition to the ominous Beansidhe, the Beantighe is friendly and warm. She is a housekeeper and watches over the animals and children in the house.

The Bean-tighe's Nature

The Bean-tighe loves a warm fire and kind-hearted humans, and she will watch over the children at night. Irish folklore tells of mothers getting up in the middle of the night to check on the children and found the children had an extra blanket covering them or a window open/closed to adjust the temperature in the room. This was the work of the Bean-tighe. The Bean-tighe loves cream and berries, and therefore should be offered such.

Don't Keep Your House TOO Clean!

Other tales tell of old Irish women who were careful not to keep their homes too clean, for fear of being accused of having a Bean-tighe. During the Witch Trial era, if you were thought to be a friend of the fairies, you were often accused of witchcraft. If you are of Milesian descent, the Bean-tighe will be more likely to take up residence in your home, but she has been known to help those who call her.

Some Say the Bean-tighe Isn't a "REAL" Irish Fairy

Sure, the first "source" to talk about the Irish house fairy, the bean-tighe, was WY Evans-Wentz. Here's the excerpt from his book The Fairy Faith in Celtic Countries:

The Bean-Tighe.[25]—'The Bean-tighe, the fairy housekeeper of the enchanted submerged castle of the Earl of Desmond, is supposed to appear sitting on an ancient earthen monument shaped like a great chair and hence called Suidheachan, the "Housekeeper's Little Seat," on Knock Adoon (Hill of the Fort), which juts out into the Lough. The Bean-tighe, as I have heard an old peasant tell the tale, was once asleep on her Seat, when the Buachailleen[26] or "Little Herd Boy" [Pg 82]stole her golden comb. When the Bean-tighe awoke and saw what had happened, she cast a curse upon the cattle of the Buachailleen, and soon all of them were dead, and then the "Little Herd Boy" himself died, but before his death he ordered the golden comb to be cast into the Lough.'[27]

Some modern "fairy authors" claim this story by Evans-Wentz doesn't refer to a fairy at all but simply the "woman of the house" or may even be a mistaken identity for a bean-sidhe (banshee) instead. I tend not to question folklorists who have long since been dead and of whom also traveled the countryside collecting their stories and anecdotes. And of who graduated from such esteemed universities like Oxford. I also tend to go with their word over modern bloggers who are self-proclaimed "experts" on the field of fae and Irish language. But that's just me. You can make up your own mind.

3. The Boggart: The Bad House Elf

The Boggart was a Scottish house elf that you did not want in your home. His other names are hobgoblin, goblin, boogie man, and gob. They are similar in appearance to the Brownie; however, in a more distorted form. Some believe he is a Brownie gone bad. If you have a Brownie in your home and do not treat him well, he may turn into a Boggart. Boggarts will eat the wood that makes up a home, like a large termite, and destroy the foundation of a home if not exorcised. Another theory is the Boggart could also be a relative of the Ballybog (a peat bog fairy). The Boggart also torments the household, particularly picking on the children. They steal the food from a child's plate and try to smother them in the middle of the night. This is where the image of the Boogieman originated.

4. Bwbachs: The Welsh Cottager Fairy

Bwbachs (pronounced boo-box) are Welsh solitary house fairies that live in Welsh homes. They are protective of the house; however, they do not help with chores and can become a nuisance. Their mischievous nature lends them the ability to chase off anyone who they feel threatens the household, which could include friendly neighbors, friends, and even family members. They are tiny men who wear red hats and loincloths. Keep them happy by leaving offerings of food (traditionally bread) and keeping the house warm. To distract them from running off your houseguests, keep the milk and bread out and stoke up the fire. Other names for the bwbachs are cottagers and booakers.

5. The Monaciello

House fairies (and fairies in general) are traditionally known to enjoy a good drink, and wine is no exception. The Monaciello is an Italian house fairy who enjoys a good drink so much that he will move into your wine cellar. He will protect your wine cellar when given wine offerings regularly. His name means "little monk" because he wears a red monk's hood. The monaciello is always drunk, but typically very friendly. Folklore tells stories of Monaciello guarding a wine cellar, but also guarding a sacred treasure. If you can steal Monaciello's hood, you can take his treasure.

6. The Clurichaun

The Clurichaun is a cousin of the Leprechaun in Ireland. He looks exactly like a Leprechaun except for the fact that he wears red and is another of the house elves. He drinks a lot of wine and lives in wine cellars; however, he is never sloppy and always well-groomed. His job, which he's taken upon himself, is to watch over the wine cellar and make sure there are no leaks or wine going bad. Give him a bit of your wine on a regular basis, and he will remain happy and friendly. Ignore him or mistreat him and he will empty your wine stock and leave the cellar in a catastrophic state. Folklore tells of the Clurichaun singing old Irish songs and protecting against wine thieves.

7. The Kobold: German House Elf

Like the Scottish brownie, the kobold is a German sprite who helps with the chores. The name kobold has a few translations, the most believable being "the one who rules the house". Kobolds are short, ugly beings who are depicted with large ears, hairy bodies, and large noses. They sometimes wear a cloak or dress in a suit and a large-brimmed hat. Unlike brownies, kobolds love hearing thank you and receiving gifts, particularly of clothing and food. In comparison to the brownie, the kobold will turn into a mischievous, malevolent creature if he or she feels they aren't appreciated.

The Green Man Legend

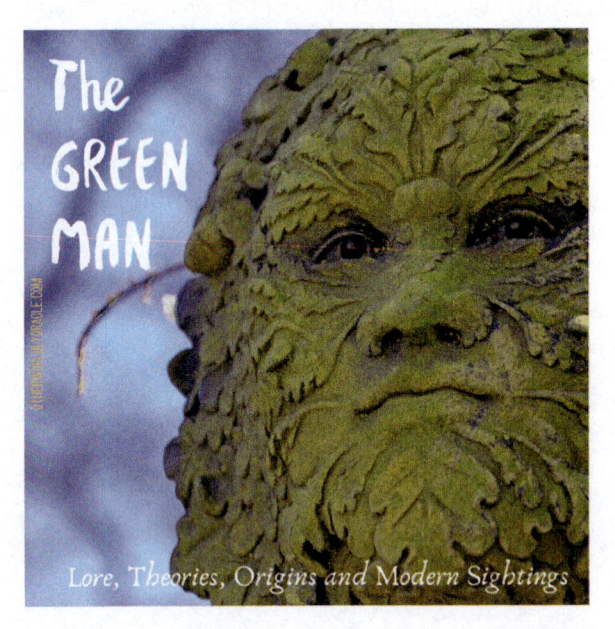

The Green Man is a forest spirit steeped in folklore dating back hundreds (possibly thousands) of years. Sources say the Green Man legend originated in Europe; however, stories and evidence circulate worldwide. If you google "The Green Man", you'll find a plethora of information on the Green Man motifs and sculptures found on churches all over Europe. But there's much more to the Green Man legend. Is this forest god merely an old pagan legend or is he real? These are the Green Man pagan origins and TRUE modern sightings.

The Green Man Legend: Pagan Origins

The first time I'd read about the Green Man, the legend grabbed my attention and didn't let go. I've always had a fascination with forest spirits, fairies, and old gods but the Green Man holds a special place in my wild heart. The Green

Man, while overlooked in modern times as a piece of garden art, was once a forest god to our pagan ancestors. He wasn't just a forest god – he was the ultimate guardian of the forest.

Who is the Green Man?

The Green Man is an omnipresent, ancient guardian of the forest. He's depicted as being a man with green skin and covered completely in foliage of various types. The most popular Green Man illustrations depict oak leaves and acorns, hawthorn leaves, and sometimes holly leaves and berries. Sometimes leaves spew from his mouth. He's an ever-present symbol of rebirth, rejuvenation, and the life and death cycle of nature. His job is to keep the woods wild – to preserve the sanctity of the forest (plants, trees, rivers, and animals) threatened by our modern advancements. He is essentially the king of the forest.

The Green Man in Architecture

Before we dive into the different architectural depictions of the Green Man, first let's talk about WHY the green man is even included on church walls and architecture. Especially since the church's goal was to "stamp out" paganism and the like. There are a couple of theories: one, that the people who built the churches still held onto their old pagan belief systems. And two that the church felt the only way to appease the old gods (or "devils") was to give them a small honorary space of their own – on the walls of the church. And yet another theory says the green men were included in the church's architecture to show the locals that the old gods were like stone and therefore conquered by the church.

The Green Man on Gothic Medieval Churches and In Graveyards

At the Chartres Cathedral in France – the Green MEN on this church's wall interestingly come in 3. Literally 3 Green

Men heads all together...seemingly like a triple deity or trinity. This Gothic church dates to 1194. Long after the Church had converted the pagans in the area. It appears like the two on either side have leaves/foliage emerging from their mouths while the middle Green Man does not. Homeboy on the left seems to have grapes in his foliage while the other two look more oak covered.

At the Exeter Cathedral in Exeter, England – built in the 12th century, around the same time as the Chartres Cathedral, this Norman Gothic church boasts at least 20 depictions of the Green Man throughout its architecture. Many of them have greenery coming out of their mouths.

The Green Man is also a popular motif in Scottish cemeteries, likely representing creation and life springing out of death. There are literally dozens of churches besides the two mentioned that feature the Green Man as a motif. Or is he more than just a design? We think so. While not a part of church architecture, it's also interesting to note that many old Inns and pubs in Britain and the U.S. are named for the Green Man (possibly a tradition linking this entity to old apothecaries that gathered herbs centuries ago OR as a forester that dressed in Green).

The Green Man Pagan God, Jack in the Green, and the Burryman

There's a theory that Green Man was once a central figure of May Day, in ancient Ireland called Beltane, a fire and fertility festival. While this theory is debated, we see a glimpse of the Green Man in figure Jack in the Green.

Jack in the Green is a man clothed in foliage and paraded in a procession on May Day in modern times. The tradition nearly died out but has seen a revival because of pagan and historical groups in England. While seemingly odd in modern times, in ancient times it was performed to ensure a bountiful crop.

A similar tradition in Scotland called the Burryman still exists, in which a man is covered in sticky burdock heads (called burries) and waltzed around town to ensure good luck for the coming year. And again, in Derbyshire, the Garland King is dressed all in flowers. The tradition of covering oneself in foliage isn't a new idea.

The Wild Men of the Woods

The Green Man myth mirrors various woodland creatures and gods. In fact, he may be the same or may have inspired the legends of other similar beings such as the Wild Men of the Woods (AKA woodwose, wodwose, wudwas), the horned god Cernunnos, and Greek forest spirits called fauns.

Wildmen of the Woods are forest beings whose origins are now somewhat shrouded in mystery – just like the Green Man. They were men who lived in the forest, covered in hair, with an otherworldly wisdom. Wildmen of the Woods might have once been pagan gods, demonized by the Church, who have fallen into the category of "folklore" after their cults fell under the pressure of conversion. With the Dark Ages, people were warned of going too deep into the woods for fear of encountering beasts, fairies, and wild men. Were these Wildmen of the Woods the German versions of the Romans' fauns? Were they the same as the Green Man?

Is Sasquatch the Green Man?

Being that the Wild Men of the Woods, aka the Woodwose, were hair-covered men who lived deep in the woods and were often seen with leaves and branches stuck or woven through their hair, couldn't this possibly be a link to the Sasquatch of American legend? Sure, sasquatch has gotten a bad rap over the years mainly due to charlatans faking their existence for a few bucks. But Native peoples of the Pacific Northwest have legends about the sasquatch and how he is essentially a guardian of the forest. We see similar beliefs with the Himalayan Yeti – an ape-like creature who guards the Himalayan mountains of Tibet. Another name for the Yeti being Migoi, which translates to "Wild Man".

Robin of the Merry Greenwood

Robin Hood, also called Robin of the Merry Greenwood, has been linked to the Green Man. Citing the website LeftLion, "Robin was not so much the vigilante hero he is thought of today, being more reminiscent of capricious pagan fairies and goblins. Popular until the reign of Elizabeth I, festivalgoers would often dress as this embodiment of misrule and mirth, with men riotously tearing about town. One case from 1492, cited by the folklorist J.C. Holt, sees a group of young men dressed as Robin and his entourage, defending their drunken behavior by claiming that acting in such a manner was a long-standing tradition, turning an intoxicated spree into the preservation of cultural heritage."

Let us note that Robin is known to wear green and is "of the forest". And the legend of the green man is ubiquitous to the same area of England from which Robin Hood emerges.

The Fauns and Cernunnos

Fauns are a Roman mythological creature mirroring the Wild Men of the Woods. The difference between the two was the faun's goat-like features. The faun has goat legs, cloven hooves, and tail. But make no mistake – both were hairy beasts that lived in the forests. Both were feared and revered. Very similar to the Green Man (except the Green Man was covered in leaves instead of hair).

Cernunnos

I'd also like to point out the legend and cult of Cernunnos – the horned god of the Celts. Again, we have a being who was lord of the forest, who bore horns on his head whose evidence is seen all over Europe. I'm not the first to make the comparison between fauns and Cernunnos, nor am I the first to compare Cernunnos to the Green Man legend. For they ALL represent that primal, wild part of man who was once so deeply connected to nature. They ALL symbolize the untouched parts of the forest that refuse to be tamed. They are ALL fertile, virile creatures with a love for the wild. And while most of us see these beings as fantasy, they were once more than that.

Modern Green Man Sightings

There have been numerous green man sightings in modern times, leaving us to wonder if the Green Man is more than a mythical figure. Via the Sasquatch Chronicles, a man in England recalls his Green Man sighting as a boy. He and his friends were putting up a swing in the woods, where he encountered a seven-foot-tall man with long hair cloaked in leaves. He believes this to be the Green Man and still has nightmares about it. There are those who believe Big Foot might also be the Green Man or at least in the same "family". People who see Big Foot also claim he's covered in leaves! I'll lead you back to the section on the Wildmen of the Woods for further conclusions.

In a recent trip to the Blue Ridge Mountains of Georgia, my mom and I snapped some random photos of the woods near our cabin. We could literally feel the presence of nature spirits all around us. While it was exciting, it was also unnerving, and we felt a little paranoid at one point. After looking at the photos taken of the woods that night, a large, leafy face emerged – the Green Man. I believe he is either one of many forest spirits, or he is the same spirit that is omnipresent in the world's forests. He is the protector of wildlife and will make his presence known if he feels you're threatening his forest.

The Connection Between Fairies and Witches

Today fairies are not just for little girls' imagination, they're for witches and magical practitioners too. But it's not truly anything new. It dates to at least ancient times. There are many historical and folkloric connections between fairies and witches particularly in European traditions. Let's learn about this connection, as well as where and how the first witch made friends with the fae.

First, Let's Define the Fae (As Best We Can)

For the intent of this post, I'll be referring to the fae from an European traditional perspective. Keep in mind there are spirits similar or comparable to the fae all over the world in nearly every ancient, magical tradition. Just as there are mermaids in many cultures worldwide. For this post, I'm sticking to the fae of my personal ancestors, as this is where my knowledge lies currently.

So, what are the fae, exactly? Can we even define them if we tried? The fae, also called faeries or fairies, have many names and many faces. We'll see a large variation in temperament, appearance, folklore, traditions, etc. as we travel from country to country and region to region across the European continent. But if I had to define the fae, I'd say they are spirits or otherworldly beings that permeate Celtic lore. Sometimes they seem to be attached to natural landmarks, other times they are attached to homes, families or even individuals. They've even been known to attach to especially magical individuals.... like witches.

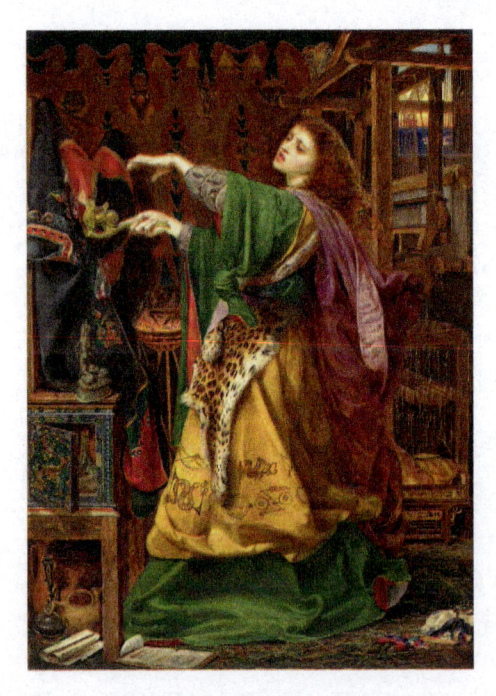

Morgan Le Fay: The "First" Fairy Witch

Ever heard of King Arthur and the Knights of the Round Table? Within the legends of Camelot are stories of a powerful and feared "fairy witch". Her name is Morgan Le Fay, and in some versions of the Arthurian legend, she is King Arthur's sister. The last two words of her name Le Fay literally means the fairy. Morgan Le Fay lived in Avalon and had many psychic and supernatural abilities, and so was accused of being a fairy and a witch by those who didn't live on the Isle. And likely because of Christian influence in the Arthurian mythos.

Morgan Le Fay and the Isle of Avalon

Different versions of the Arthurian legend paint her in different lights. Morgan Le Fay is a paradoxical character, as are most powerful females in the old myths. Depending on the version of the story, she was either Arthur's downfall or his healer and savior. The Morgan-friendly legends depict her taking Arthur to the Isle of Avalon, to be his last resting place. Moreover, the Isle of Avalon was a magical place beyond the mist and inhabited by fairies. Nine magical sisters lived there, Morgan Le Fay being one of the nine. Sometimes the Lady of the Lake is one of the nine sisters and in other stories Morgan is the Lady of the Lake herself.

The Fairy Witch Trials

We have all heard of the unspeakable horrors that took place with the Witch Trials in Europe and America. Superstition, power-hunger, and patriarchal greed drove these massacres to abundance. But what most people don't know is fairies played a part in the Witch Trials too.

The Fisherwife of Palermo

Most of the Fairy Witch Trials took place in Italy. Out of the known sixty-five cases, the Fisherwife of Palermo's fairy witch trial in Sicily was most well-known. The wife of a fisherman claimed she could leave her body behind and party with the elves whenever she wanted. She explained the King and Queen of Elves promised her riches and other pleasures if she denounced all other gods. She signed a contract and, on many occasions, spiritually joined the elves in feasting and revelry. The fairy faith was strong, and most believed the Fisherwife to be associated with fairies and not the Devil. So inevitably, they released her. Her accusers agreed she was merely "having dreams" of fairies and not physically copulating with "devils".

Isobel Gowdie & the Queen of Elfame

In a witch trial in Scotland, an accused witch claimed she'd met with the Queen of Fairies (the Queen of Elfame) under the hills. Isobel Gowdie said the fairies taught her and other women how to fly on beanstalks to meet with other witches. Isobel's confession is the most detailed account from this time. And can be researched in its entirety online. I also recommend reading Emma Wilby's book "The Visions of Isobel Gowdie."

Besse Dunlop, Fairy Witch of Lynn

Besse or Bessie Dunlop of Lynn was a woman accused of witchcraft in North Ayrshire, Scotland in the sixteenth century. The trial documents claim Besse Dunlop confessed to having a familiar spirit named Tom Reid, the ghost of a soldier who aided her prophecies and gave her healing remedies with which to make a living. She also confessed to visiting Elfame (elf-land) through an ancient cave. The Queen of Elfame supposedly sent Besse her familiar Thomas to help her as she was in a dire situation at the time.

The Nature of the Fairies

Fairies were such an integral part of folklore in Europe that most people didn't associate fairies with the Christian devil for many years. Often, as in the case of the Fisherwife of Palermo, the Church allowed the accused to go free. The Church explained these women's experiences with fairies as simply dreams or mental illness. However, if fairies were mentioned in alignment with the Devil or familiars, or if the accused was thought to have harmed another using witchcraft, they were tried/tortured/executed.

The Celtic and Germanic People and Household Fae

As an elderly woman in Ireland, local custom held that you shouldn't keep your house too clean. Otherwise, people would be suspicious of a bean-tighe in your home. A bean-tighe (pronounced ban-tee) was a female fairy like the

Scottish brownie who tended house and watched over the children. They accused old women of witchcraft, particularly with fairies involved. The kobold is a Germanic household fairy or dwarf that's known to take up residence in a home and aid in the household chores. These household types seem to be more prevalent among magical or royal people.

Cunningfolk and Fairy Friends

In opposition to witches who practiced maleficium, there were others who practiced "white" magic. The local cunningman or cunningwoman healed, counteracted curses, helped find lost objects and performed other helpful magical tasks. Many of the cunningfolk received their otherworldly knowledge from the fairies.

Biddy Early

An Irish woman by the name of Biddy Early was a cunningwoman and "fairy doctor" who lived in the late 1700's through the 1800's. Biddy was called upon to not only heal people but to find lost items, to cure sick animals, and to aid in crop abundance. Biddy was well known for her herbal knowledge and for clairvoyance. Some said Biddy Early was given powers by the fairies, and that she carried a "fairy bottle" that told whispered the fairies' secrets to her.

Modern Fairy Witches

The cunningfolk and witches of the past are gone but not forgotten. They live on in a new wave of witches and magical practitioners reviving the old ways. Some fairy witches practice fairy witchcraft by basing their magic and beliefs on fairy lore. Others follow a more religious form of fairy witchcraft.

The Feri Tradition

The Feri Tradition was created by Victor Anderson. This form of witchcraft is based on sensuality and can be very intense in nature. From my research it's not necessarily focused on the actual belief or working with fairies, but more on an ecstatic experience within oneself. There are also various fairy Wiccan traditions that tie Celtic fairy beliefs into ritual and practice.

The Connection Between Fairies and Witches: Natural and Ancestral Theories

I have a few theories as to why fairies and intricately linked to witches. I don't think there's any one answer, but it's more of a web of answers. One of the reasons there's a connection between fairies and witches is simple – nature. An undying, passionate love for nature and the preservation of it. Witches walk the path of the craft because most seek to commune with the energies all around us, radiating off of our Mother Earth.

Witches Love Nature, As Do the Fae

At least some of the fae are likely spirits of nature, so naturally when witches work with nature, they may find they are also working with elementals and the fae. When nature spirits, fairies, realize a witch is a witch who cares and is in sync with Mother Earth, they will begin teaching that witch their secrets. Is it no wonder witches were closely linked with fairies during the Witch Trials? It makes sense to me.

Fairies and Elves…They May Be Our Ancient Ancestors

Another theory is that the fae may be ancestral in origin. Shocking? It may be at first, but the more you study Celtic lore and history, as well as Norse Germanic tradition, you'll see a pattern emerging. Many of our ancient ancestors claimed descent from faeries and elven races. In Ireland and

Scotland, certain clans claim descent the Tuatha de Danann. Some say Cliodhna, Flidais, and Lugh are their ancestors (to name a few). And in Scandinavian countries, we have stories of our ancestors sacrificing to the álfar (elven beings), often on top of ancestral burial mounds. And being that many witches today seek to honor their ancestors, they are also naturally honoring the potential fae in their bloodline.

So, when our ancestors in the Medieval Age and early modern era were accused of being witches and consorting with faeries, they were also often accused of being heathens or keeping the "old pagan ways" alive. Perhaps these faeries, our ancestors' ancestors, came to those witches and pagans because they still believed. Unlike their converted counterparts.

Those Gifted With the "Sight"

In addition, in faery folklore, it was frequently said the fae would give their secrets and essentially "work" with people who had the "sight". For example, Biddy Early. Or people who had psychic and medium abilities. And, of course, it also happened these individuals with abilities would end up being accused of witchcraft and sadly end up in a courtroom, on a pyre, or hanging from a tree. And if these individuals who had the ability to talk to the fae were fighting to keep the old ways alive including to honor nature and sacred fairy sites and traditions, it makes sense the fae would be more willing to communicate with them than those who weren't.

Mermen: Old Legends, Gods, and Sightings

MERMEN LEGENDS

МОРСКІЯ СИРЕНЫ.

When you hear the term mermaid, what do you think of? I think of a red-headed teenage girl wearing a shell-bikini top with fins for legs. But to only focus our attention on the mermaids would be a dishonor to the other merpeople – the mermen. In addition to the many mermaid legends, there are just as many mermen legends. Some stories say they were ugly and mean, others remain neutral. In certain countries, mermen were benevolent. Let's explore the fascinating and sometimes frightening world of mermen. This time we're leaving Ariel out.

Ireland & Orkney Mermen: Merrows and Finmen

The merman legend penetrates cultural barriers; however, in Western Europe it was quite prevalent. In Ireland, merrows were merpeople who were both bad and good, depending on who told the tale. In the Dark Ages, male merrows were hideous, nasty creatures while the female merrows were beautiful. Male merrows were seen wearing red caps, which was thought to give them the magical ability to breathe underwater OR on land. If their cap was stolen, they would never return to the sea.

Mermen Legend: The Finfolk

Finfolk were vicious creatures, coming to the Orkney shores at certain times of the year to hunt their next victim. They would kidnap a woman. Then enslave her for eternity. The finfolk lived in an underwater place called Finfolkaheem. Silver is their weakness. To prevent from being captured by one of the finfolk, cast silver in all directions to distract the merman. Finmen are tall and skinny and have magical powers. They transform into something completely invisible so that they can sneak up on their prey.

There were also male selkies, the Bluemen of the Muir, Nixes, and the Dinny Mara. Each of these mermen have their own unique characteristics and tales.

Scottish Mermen: The Blue Men of the Minch

I can't say any other merman seems as scary as the Blue Men of the Minch. They are especially known for having violent tendencies and having fun wrecking ships along the Scottish coastline. Another name for this aggressive merman is Storm Kelpie. People believe they purposely drum up sea storms to cause wrecks and drownings. Legend has it, sailors have seen the Blue Men floating atop the water. They've often asked for poetry to be recited. And if you refuse? They'll capsize your boat. Or worse.

Ancient Mermen Gods: Gods of the Sea

While the merman legend dominated Western European folklore through the Dark Ages, the merman was present in every age. In ancient cultures, there is a myriad of gods that are half-man-half-fish.

Triton: Greek Merman God

King Triton was the father of Ariel in The Little Mermaid, but his name pre-dates Disney. Triton was an ancient Greek god of the sea. He was the son of Poseidon and Amphitrite. He caused great storms at sea and was a very erotic spirit. Some myths say he was a vicious lover. He carried a conch shell for a horn and often accompanied his father, Poseidon. He is depicted as a merman – half-man-half-fish with long hair. Shapeshifting is one of his abilities.

Glaucus

Glaucus was another merman god of the sea in ancient Greek mythology. Though his story is different than Triton's. Glaucus consumed a magical herb that inevitably led to his transformation into a sea god. He had fish-like features, and he was an advisor and protector of sailors.

The Dogon Tribe's Mermen-Gods

Our African ancestors also had their own mermen deities they call the Nommo. Interestingly, the Dogons' creation story involves the Nommo, these half-man half-fish beings, who came here from another planet thousands of years ago. Apparently, they believe they descend from these merman gods, as they are credited with the creation of man.

Enki: Sumerian God of the Sea

Enki was a Sumerian god of war and wisdom and thought to be a creator god. Other names for Enki include Lord of the Water and Ea. Sumerian mythology says Enki saved the

Earth from the Great Flood. He may manifest in the merman form.

Olokun: Orisha Sea God

To the Nigerians, Olokun was the King of the Sea and manifested in the form of a merman or serpent. Olokun is a psychopomp, leading lost souls to the other side. This is a common belief of mermen and mermaids. They often lead drowned sailors' souls to the other realm (at least the nice ones did). As a ruler of the sea, Olokun also has dominion over rivers and streams.

These are just a few of the ancient mermen gods across the world. In the Middle East, archaeologists found bronze statues and carvings of mermen that predate written history. The belief in mermen goes back thousands of years.

Mermen: Are They Good or Evil?

There are conflicting accounts of the mermen temperament towards human beings. Some legends tell of mermen who help drowning sailors. While others depict the merman as being a vampire, a human-eater or kidnapper. The merman had the ability to lead souls to the other side, but often would take pleasure in capturing the sailors' souls and keeping them in pots or cages at the bottom of the sea. Never to be freed to cross on to the other side.

A Merrow Who Collected Souls

In a story recorded by W.B. Yeats, an Irish man was friends with a male merrow (merman). They drank together and carried on as old buddies would, until one day the merrow asked the man to join him for a drink on the seabed. The man agreed and found the merrow had been keeping sailors' souls in pots. The man knew the right thing to do was to free these souls and was able to get his merrow-friend intoxicated. Then he stole his red cap, swam to the bottom of the ocean, and freed all of the captured souls. This legend gives the reader the idea that mermen were in fact malevolent towards humans.

Selkie Lovers

Male selkies of Shetney were attractive and were desired as lovers for human women. A woman could cry seven tears into the ocean and a male selkie would appear. In this light, we see mermen differently. Also, there are tales of mermen saving drowned people and taking them to shore. We have only to read the stories of Glaucus (above) and see that he was a guide to humans. So, were mermen good or evil? Are they nice or mean to humans? Or perhaps it just depends on the kind of merman or the individual merman.

"Real" Mermen Sightings

In recent years, thanks to Hollywood, there's been a resurgence of interest in mythical water creatures. Animal Planet made a "documentary" called Mermaid: A Body Found. Since then, people wonder more and more whether merpeople are real. Are they human-like sea creatures or just unidentified sea creatures? There have been some real mermen sightings in recent times, as recent as five years ago. But many of these sightings date back to the 1800's and before.

There are dozens of videos on YouTube showing viewers what the videographers claim to be "real mermen sightings". Some are rather convincing, while others are obviously humans dressed in mermen costume. Unfortunately, even the most convincing videos turn out to be fakes, due to modern technology and the ability to photoshop and animate videos.

A Merman Found

Perhaps my favorite story of a real sighting dates to the 1800's. A man in Ireland went to the shore one day and found two young mermen lying there, injured and in pain. One was dead and the other was dying. He believed they were washed to shore during a major storm on the water. The man helped the dying creature and took it home. He placed it in a tub of water and nursed it back to health. The merman would only eat shellfish and drink milk.

The Creature Released

The merman wouldn't talk to him, and his appearance was rather appalling. The young merman was three-four feet in length with the torso and head of a human boy and the bottom a fish. Its skin was green, and he had webbed fingers and seaweed-like hair. This story was published in the local newspaper. Supposedly the man released the merman back into the ocean.

Conclusion

There are stories of sailors seeing merfolk in past centuries, but not as many of these tales surface today. Is it because we've lost the belief in supernatural things, or is it because these beings have gone into complete hiding? The sad thing is, even if we found proof, people probably wouldn't believe it anyway.

King of the Fairies, Knockma Hill, and a Haunted Castle Hackett

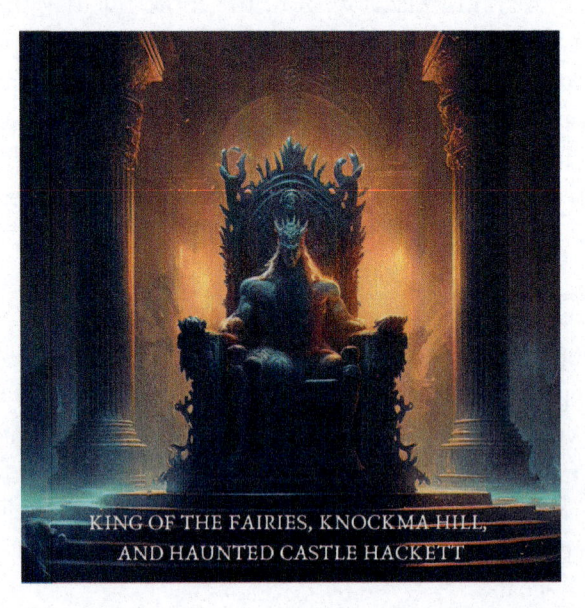

KING OF THE FAIRIES, KNOCKMA HILL, AND HAUNTED CASTLE HACKETT

I've waited my entire life to visit Ireland, and recently I had the absolute pleasure of finally going. I knew I would experience a feeling of being home, an undeniable connection I've always felt for my ancestors' homeland. And I was also hoping to visit places connected to the good folk, as they're called in Ireland. If you've never heard of good folk, a term you're probably familiar with is fairy. Well, not only did I visit a legitimate fairy forest, but I came across the home of the King of the Fairies in Galway. Read on to hear my true-life fairy tale and discover why you should put Knockma Hill and Castle Hackett on your travel list!

First, Who is the King of the Fairies?

The King of the Fairies of Connacht, as he's known in Galway, is also known by his name Finvarra (Finn Bheara). He appears in numerous Irish tales and legends, namely in the

Fenian Cycle in early Irish literature and in the The Feast of the House of Conán circa the fifteenth century.

Fionnbharr of the Fenian Cycle is believed to be the same mythical figure as the King of the Fairies of Connacht, yet some scholars believe they could be separate. Finvarra, according to Edain McCoy's A Witch's Guide to Faery Folk, is one of the Tuatha de Danann. If you don't already know, the Tuatha de Danann are a race of ancient gods that inhabited the Emerald Isle before the Milesians invaded. They have since also been called the "good folk" and are considered a race of fairies, by some. Finvarra is a King of the Tuatha and is known to "enjoy the games of Hurling and chess and has his favorite human opponents."

King Finvarra Kidnaps a Bride

Apparently, this King of the Fairies has no quams with humans and enjoys their company. Particularly young women. In one Knockma Hill tale, Finvarra steals a human bride named Ethna for his lover. The lord from which she's been taken hunts down her whereabouts and is told to dig down into Knockma Hill to find his new bride. So, he does just that and then spreads salt over the earth. His bride is returned to him. Once he has Ethna in his possession, he notices she's enspelled…singing to herself, never speaking, sleeping a lot, and generally in a daze. According to the Library Ireland, the spell is broken when a fairy girdle is removed from her waist and thrown into the fire.

They say you can still see the place where the lord dug to recover his enchanted bride on Knockma Hill. But I promise you, it's not as easy as it sounds. Once you are there, things are rather hazy…almost like there's an enchantment over the entire wood that keeps one from locating a doorway to King Finvarra's world.

The King of the Fairies is also King of the Dead?

I want to bring up a theory of mine that I'm currently researching for a future book. And that is that the elves and fairies are the dead. Our ancestors. Why am I bringing this up in relation to the King of the Fairies of Connacht? Well, they also say Finvarra is the King of the Dead. And, as there are ancient mesolithic tombs and people buried on Knockma Hill, the correlation is too much to ignore. We see ancient burial tombs and cairns all over the ancient world, particularly in Celtic and Norse regions, that are also said to be elven and fairy haunts. And the fact that the fairies in Ireland reside in the hills and mounds, as do the dead, I believe says it all.

What and Where is Knockma Hill and Wood?

Knockma Hill, also known as Knockma Wood, is a small, preserved forest in County Galway in Ireland. It's located in the town of Belclare, but most people know the area because of the larger town called Tuam. Though both Belclare and Tuam are small compared to big cities like Dublin. This ancient hill has a long history of being inhabited by early humans in Ireland (circa 7000 BCE according to archaeological finds) and is also incredibly rich in local fairy folklore. Interestingly, the sign at the trail says it is part of Caherlistrane, Co. Galway. You will find it on the GPS and Google Maps by simply looking up Knockma Hill in Galway, or by coordinates 53.4841° N, 8.9664° W.

Knockma Hill has been used for ceremonial purposes and burials for thousands of years. As early as 7000 BCE. And there are supposedly burial chambers and tunnels within the hill itself. Though these seem to be completely hidden or buried under earth and rock in modernity. There are four larger confirmed cairns, which mark ancient burial sites, on top of the hill that can be seen today. Two burial chambers and the remnants of a hill fort were also recently discovered by archaeologists Nora Brennan and Michael Gibbons, according to the Irish Times. Brennan and Gibbons claim this site is as important to Ireland's history as Newgrange.

The Otherworldly Hike around Knockma

Knockma Hill is heavily forested and there are hiking trails encircling it. In fact, there is one large easy trail labeled on the map as Green (the Forest trail), which makes a circle around the hill and back down it. In addition, there's a blue trail and a red trail. The blue trail is labeled as Finvarra's trail and the red as Queen Medb's. This is because the blue supposedly leads to Finvarra's castle and the red to Queen Medb's cairn at the top of Knockma Hill. As you enter the forest trails, specifically the beginning of the Green trail, you'll notice a sign that says Coill Chnoc Mea, Knockma Wood.

Before we even entered Knockma Wood, we could feel the earth around us pulsing and radiating. The otherworldly energy literally rose from the ground and swirled around us in never-ending spirals of wind, leaves, and sheep's brays. Like most of Ireland, a sheep and dairy farm lie at the base of Knockma Hill. These sacred creatures by no means take away from the faery vibes of the forest. As we entered the forest and began climbing the Forest trail, we noticed moss-covered trees, abundant ferns, and a cool breeze. A large expanse of oak, beech, maples, and other trees I couldn't identify blanketed the blue sky.

There were other people hiking and enjoying the beautiful preserve with their friends and family members, but that also didn't take away from the experience. I ate up every single moment of the hike, but I had one major mission – to find Queen Maeve's Cairn and Finvarra's Castle. We would have to take the higher climb, the more moderate trails, to find them.

Queen Maeve's Cairn, Finvarra's Castle, and David's Bed

After an exhilarating (though somewhat challenging) climb up the hill, we reached a clearing where the trees faded away and allowed us to see one of the most gorgeous views I've ever witnessed. They say on top of Knockma Hill, you can see nearly all of Galway. And I would believe that. Look at the photos and you'll see, but truly the photos didn't even do it justice. Not far past the lookout area, we discovered a fork in the trail where we could either stay on the Green trail or take the Blue trail to Finvarra's Castle and the Cairns. We immediately turned right and headed up the trail in search of the King of the Fairies and Queen Medb.

The further you climb up Knockma Hill, the rockier and wilder it gets. Plants with thorny stems seem to cover the rocky outcroppings, and when I noticed these, I remembered the late Edain McCoy saying where there are thorny and spiny plants there are malevolent fairies. Further, we approached Queen Medb's hill and cairn with caution and with respect. We came to the very top of the red trail (which branches off the blue) to find a park bench situated in front of a stone wall, of sorts. We figured this must be Queen Medb's cairn. But there were no signs and we didn't feel it would be welcome to climb on top of the stone wall or piles. I felt a strong amount of energy emanating from this place. We attempted to walk up a stone pile but didn't go very far, again out of respect for those buried there and for the Queen herself.

The First Rule of Fairy Club…You Don't Talk About Fairy Club

Further down the trail, we ran into a lovely elderly couple. I asked them about the stone walls and houses and the woman said, "oh you know there were people that once lived up here." And the elderly man said, "there's a man buried on top of Knockma Hill." I found it interesting how they refrained from mentioning King Finvarra, fairies, or Queen Medb. I've been told the Irish people today don't like talking about the wee folk. We walked further and came across what appeared to be remnants of small stone houses. We assume this is what is referred to as Finvarra's Castle, but again…there were no signs or markers telling us.

David's Bed

Walking onward and returning to the forest, we came across another ruined stone house with a sign in front. I couldn't read the Gaelic words at the time but came home and translated them. It says "David's bed". I wonder who is David and why is his name associated with this ruined stone cottage? The energy there was palpable...And directly behind David's bed is a ridge with hauntingly beautiful trees. And a path that runs next to a large stone wall that has since been overtaken by moss. You can't even tell their stone unless you walk right up to them. In addition to this finding, there are newly carved and cleverly placed wooden carvings done by a local woodworker/artist. They are of local animals like the badger, fox, and owl, and some are fun fairy homes. Someone had also made a large natural mandala at the base of David's bed that we admired for quite some time.

Fairies Haunt Castle Hackett

It's not just Knockma Hill and wood that will capture your soul and imagination. It's the captivating ruined towerhouse at the base of the hill known as Castle Hackett. Castle Hackett was built sometime in the thirteenth century by a Norman family called the Hacketts. The Kirwans took over the castle in the fifteenth century and intermarried with the Hacketts. The Castle towerhouse was abandoned in the eighteenth century and lies in ruin today. There's a large chunk missing out of one of the walls (at least) and no roof. And it is covered in foliage. While in ruin, it is a breathtaking site to see.

According to WB Yeats, the Hacketts claimed to be descendants of a fairy. And I wonder if they claim any relation to King Finvarra, but I couldn't find a solid resouce to back that up. The Hacketts were known to have the "sight" and had dealings with the fairies on Knockma Hill. It's no wonder, since the Castle is situated within feet of the fairy forest. Local legends say King Finvarra and his fairies haunt the ruined towerhouse today. And the locals also say you can see the fairies waging war in the sky above Knockma Hill. This was a sight many locals bore witness to during the Great Potato Famine.

Castlehackett Manor House: Its History, Fairies, and Staying There Today

After Castle Hackett was abandoned in the eighteenth century, the family built a large manor house with three stories nearby in 1703. It is called Castlehackett House and still stands today. In fact, it's been converted into a lovely Bed and Breakfast and you can book a room or suite there through Airbnb. The history attached to the Manor House is also a tumultous and interesting one. John Kirwan, the man who built the house, was said to have been haunted by the fairies of Knockma. One story goes that John was preparing his horse for a race in Galway, when a little man walked down from Knockma Hill and approached him at the stable. He told John that if he allowed the little people to ride his horse for him in Galway the next day, that he would surely win the race. John agreed and, sure enough, one of the little people showed up in Galway for everyone to see, rode John's horse, and won the race.

In 1923, it was bombed during the Civil War, and the third level was destroyed. Then it was rebuilt in 1929 with two stories remaining. It is a charming and peaceful place to stay, and I highly recommend it! Plus, the owner Joyce McDonagh makes a mean Irish breakfast. We found it fascinating that the "Do's and Dont's" of listed in our suite states "Don't be afraid of ghosts…only good spirits reside here!" While we stayed at Castlehackett House, we experienced nothing spooky whatsoever. I truly believe Joyce is right…if there are spirits there, they are benevolent. If you decide to visit, bring warm pajamas as it does get cold at night. And be sure to walk around the property and enjoy the view of Knockma Hill nearby. And…don't let yourself be taken by the King of the Fairies.

Part II: Fairy Magick and Mischief

Attract Fairies To Your Home & Garden

Fairies are spirits that often haunt natural places like rivers, mountains, forests, and fields. Believe it or not, there are ways to attract fairies to your home or garden. Fairies appreciate people who protect nature, and who are spiritually in tune with the earth. But they can be finicky and mischievous, so you must be careful what kind of fairy you're inviting into your life. If you want a fairy that helps with housework or helps your garden grow, read on to learn how to attract fairies using fairy offerings and more.

First, What Are Fairies?

There are many theories as to what fairies are. I don't know if anyone has the answer. Some people say they are fallen gods, once mighty and powerful, that have been diminished into tiny spirits over the years. Others say they are the spirits of nature – the consciousness and souls of plants, trees, and landscape. Truly, I believe they are something "other" than anything we can explain or comprehend. They are otherworldly beings, spirits. But I also believe they can manifest in the physical. This makes them extraordinarily powerful.

Caution: Attract Fairies of the Nice Kind

Not every fairy is safe to invite to your home or garden, so be cautious. In fact, even the "safe" fairies can turn on you. You see, fairies don't have the same rules or morals as humans. They have their own set of rules and probably none. But for our intents and purposes, there are certain fairies that tend to be mostly benevolent and mostly malevolent. The fae you'll want to stay away from include bogles, hobgoblins, spriggans, kelpies, giants, nixies, and trolls. In addition, there were also fairies who enjoyed eating humans, like trolls, Jenny Greenteeth, the Glaistig, and giants. Check out Edain McCoy's book, A Witch's Guide to the Faery Folk to learn more about the temperament of each type of fairy.

Mostly benevolent fairies include garden fairies, brownies, gnomes, pixies, dryads, clurichauns, the monaciello, and the bean-tighe. Flower and earth fairies like pixies and gnomes are best for the garden; they protect the trees and plants and help them grow. House fairies like the brownie and bean-tighe are great to invite into your home. They will help keep it clean, prosperous, and safe. But a word to the wise – if you double cross any of these fairies, they can and will turn on you. Please do further research on the specific kind of fairy you'd like to work with before inviting them into your space.

Fairy Offerings

From Edain McCoy's Guide to the Faery Folk, "Most faeries hate profuse displays of thanks from humans whom they have helped. It is best not to utter thanks at all, but to leave out extra portions of milk, butter, or bread for them by way of showing your appreciation. These offerings are called libations…"

Milk and Dairy Offerings for the Fay

The custom of leaving libations for fairies dates back centuries. Milk farmers in Ireland would leave out a libation after every milking to keep the faeries happy. A fed, happy fairy was less likely to cause trouble on the farm. Libations of mead or bowls of barley were also common fairy offerings. For house fairies, leave a portion of your dinner on the dinner table at night. Fairies are finicky and mostly don't like to be thanked or doted over, so quietly leave your fairy offerings in your house or garden. This is a key step to attract fairies to your garden and home.

Fairy Food and Libations:

Traditionally, fairies loved sweets so anything you've baked at home is a perfect fairy offering. If you offer fruit, make sure it is organic. If the birds and ants won't eat the fruit, neither will the fairies. They also love traditional offerings like milk, wine, ale, cream, and mead. More on Fairy Foods in the next section.

Other Offerings

In addition to food offerings, the fairies are appreciative of shiny things. Ever had a necklace go missing then turn up somewhere completely obvious? This was probably a mischievous fairy! Sparkly offerings like jewelry, crystals, stones, and sea glass are appropriate. I've also cast a knot spell using purple cord, seashells, bells, and feathers to attract fairies. You can read my entire fairy knot spell here. Fairies like Celtic flute music, tinkly windchimes, and people who care for the earth and wildlife. So, make your gardening ventures an offering to the fay.

What NOT To Do When Trying to Attract the Fae

Yes, there are things you can do to attract the fae to your garden and home, but there's also things you shouldn't do. Here's a quick rundown:

- Don't hang horseshoes above your doors
- Don't put iron anywhere you want the fairies to visit/reside (the exception here, I've found, is that household fairies don't mind cast iron skillets in the kitchen)

- There shouldn't be any salt sprinkled around your house or in the garden (the exception here is the Slavic hearth spirit the Domovoi, who prefers salt as an offering)
- Deep, loud bells aren't preferred and sometimes scare the garden fairies away (it reminds them of church bells to which they are averse)
- No clergymen should reside in the home (fairies are known not to get along with officials from the church)
- If you're lazy, the fairies might get annoyed with you
- NEVER insult the fae lest they turn on you
- Don't give your typical household elves like brownies any clothing…they will leave
- Don't thank them for their help or presence

Where to Place the Fairy Offerings

If you are trying to attract a garden fairy, place the fairy offering at your garden gate or just inside the gate. Leave it on a stump, rock, or shell (something natural). Leave it out overnight and especially on one of the high holy Celtic days like Beltane or Midsummer. If you're trying to invite a house fairy into your home, you'll want to start by leaving fairy offerings on your front or back doorstep. After a few times you can leave them inside your door. Then in your kitchen or close to wherever you'd like the fairy to reside (kitchen, hallway, guest room, attic, etc). Don't be disheartened if the food or drink doesn't "disappear". That doesn't mean the fairy offering wasn't accepted.

In the Garden

Fairies are picky about where they live and visit. They can often be found in unspoiled parts of nature. If you have a gardener or lawn service, take over the duty yourself. Garden fairies don't like to be disturbed by people other than the ones they know. Add a small fountain or waterfall to your garden if budget allows. If you happen to have a stump of an old tree, this can become the fairies' sacred space. Or arrange a circle of stones. Circles are a favorite hang-out spot for fairies. Create fairy houses out of bird houses and other natural materials and place them in a safe spot in the garden. Leave offerings there for the garden fairies. Make sure no one disturbs this area.

In the Home

Fairy offerings, as detailed above, are necessary to attract a brownie or house fairy. Make sure there are no bells, high chimes, or anything with a sharp noise. No iron horseshoes should hang above the doors (fairies have an aversion to iron). There shouldn't be any mirrors in the kitchen or low to the ground. Make a special place for the brownie or house fairy to reside – an empty cabinet, pantry, closet, or shelf will do. Set up this space comfortably, like you plan to sleep there. Small pillows, blankets, and natural decorations are perfect for a brownie's space.

Contact with the Fae Through Meditation

There are other ways to get in touch with the fairy realm. Fairy offerings are helpful and potent but reaching out psychically is important. I've met numerous fairies in another state of mind – through meditation, trance, the hypnogogic/hypnopompic state and in dreams. If you don't know how to alter your mind, now's the time to start practicing and learning about it. First, try out guided meditations. Learning how to slow down your mind and open up to the universe is step number one.

Meeting the Fae in Dreams

Next, learn how to lucid dream. A lucid dream is when you're conscious in the dream and can make decisions on where to go, what to do, and even who to meet. Some say a lucid dream is different than traveling in the astral, but I believe they are one in the same. As did the ancients. If you could dream, you could meet the gods, fairies, and ancestors. Keep a dream journal and start recording your dreams every morning. Soon you'll find you're recalling dreams nearly ever day and you'll start having the ability to become conscious. Then you can meet the fae in the other realms. Just make sure to never eat their food.

Once you've met the fairies in your dreams, you can invite them to your space. Be sure to set up ground rules, though, and always ground yourself after intense experiences with the fae in the dream world.

Fairy Foods: What DO Fairies Eat?

According to Celtic lore, you must NEVER take food from a fairy or while traveling in fairyland. Else ye be stuck there forever! But what if we want to appease the faeries living in our own homes? Or the fae in our gardens? Follow us on a journey to the enchanting realm of the fae and learn what foods and libations they most prefer, according to tradition, and our modern take on ancient recipes. Including a clarification on fairy bread, fairy cakes, and much more!

First, What is Fairy Food?

You might notice if you type "fairy food" into your Google machine, it comes back with a cornucopia of frilly, froo-froo fairy cupcakes, children's birthday cakes, and other nonsensical sprinkled fodder. But here's the truth of the matter, fairies might like anything sweet, but fairy food is food that's traditionally fed to or provided to us by the faeries in Celtic fairy tales, folklore, and oral tradition. You might have also noticed the cook (Mr. Kobold) and kitchen witch

122

(Mumma Kitty) at the Otherworldly Oracle Kitchen don't just believe in the fae...they know them...intimately.

Keep in mind, it truly depends on the type of fae what fairy food they prefer. Not only the type of fae but also the region and the people living in that region. We will explore folkloric fairy food offerings from the British Isles, Ireland, Central and Eastern Europe.

A List of Typical Fairy Foods:

- Milk
- Cream
- Butter
- Ale
- Mead
- Bread
- Honey cakes
- Sweets
- Fresh Fruit
- Honey
- Water
- Herbs
- Tea
- Mushrooms
- Meats (sometimes – depends on the fairy)
- Salt (VERY rarely – depends on the fairy. Read more under Russia below)

Fairy Food Across Europe

There are many similarities across ancient cultures, regions, and modern lore from the British Isles all the way to Eastern Europe. But don't let the similarities fool you into thinking a kobold from Germany likes the same food as the Slavic

Domovoy. ALWAYS do your research before attempting to offer fairy food to the fae themselves! While the Domovoy enjoys offerings of salt, many other household faeries steer clear. Some are even warded off by salt.

Ireland

In Ireland, the fairy faith has continued for centuries. Some folks leave offerings for their household faeries, while others still acknowledge the trooping fairies that ride by their homes on the high holy days. According to Edain McCoy in A Witch's Guide to Faeries, fresh butter is a preferred food, especially in the Spring. I'd venture to say the fae would enjoy herbed butter with fresh rosemary and thyme. Add saffron to nearly any fairy food and they'll rejoice! McCoy also states to give the fae a little of each of your sabbat feasts AND the last fruit of any harvest from your garden. In addition, leave some food behind following your full moon esbats.

Fairy Fruits

Nearly every Celtic fae enjoys fresh fruit, specifically apples. The apple is a fruit featured frequently in Irish Celtic mythology, particularly on Immramma (journeys) to the Celtic Otherworld. It is an otherworldly, enchanted fruit that often heals and provides vitality to weary sailors and heroes. In the ancient tale of Cian's Son Teigue, the fairy queen Cliodhna offers Teigue and his men sustenance from a magical apple tree. She tells him this sacred tree "sustains us all", which we can assume is the faeries and all elemental creatures on her island in the Celtic Otherworld. The apple was brought to this earthly plane from the other realm. Who knows if that was intentional, for the seeds do contain a tiny bit of poison – hydrogen cyanide.

Fairy Milk

Milk is a traditional fairy food in nearly every region and culture. It seems to be ubiquitous in the fairy faith. Interestingly, in milk we find a story of the fairies giving humans food. Once there was a fairy cow, an otherworldly cow given to Ireland by the faeries, that produced a limitless supply of milk. But the fairy cow was specifically given to the people to help feed the poor. Unfortunately, the people took advantage and eventually the fairy cow was taken away because of their greed and gluttony. But fairies will ALWAYS enjoy a cup or saucer of milk from us. (Summarized from Lenihan and Green's "Meeting the Other Crowd").

NOTE: Any food left out overnight is now in the fairies' domain and MUST NEVER be consumed after!

Britain: Fairy Bannocks and Cream

In Cornwall, it's said to never scold a child who has spilled the milk. The people see it as a gift to the faeries. Hence comes the renowned phrase, "don't cry over spilled milk." You shan't cry if it appeases the good folk! In Scotland, an ancient dish called bannocks is a common fairy food offered to all types of household spirits, trooping fairies, and the like. The household Brownie is known to adore this oatmeal flatcake. Throughout the Isles, it was traditional to set a bowl of cream or milk on the windowsill or doorstep for the fae. But it was crucial to never watch for the fairies to come around. Else you anger them. And we wouldn't want that, would we?

What Fairies Eat in Eastern Europe & Russia

We know that fairies are worldwide. And Eastern Europe and Russia are no strangers to the wee folk. They just have different names and temperaments.

In Latvia and Estonia

In Latvia, Christmas is a big deal. And has been for years. A tradition of the elders in a family placing a pig's head, beer, and bread in the bija (barn) for the master of the house is still a practice for some. This takes place on Christmas Eve to appease the Majas kungs (masters of the house). There is some speculation as to whether the masters of the house are ancestors, spirits of the land or fairies. But, then again, you'll notice a lot of blurred lines with the spirits and wee folk in nearly every culture.

In Estonia, the people feed a piece of bread and drip a few drops of water or wine onto the ground for the "invisible spirit". In many cultures, giving the fae folk a bit of whatever meal they're eating was commonplace in the old days.

Fairy Food in Russia

Just as dairy is a staple food in Ireland, it's also a staple in Russia. And when the fairies are feeling extra mischievous or have been angered, they tend to mess with the peoples' dairy supply. Which, as you can guess, causes some distress. The fae will spoil milk, ruin the butter, and are even prone to stealing cheese and yogurt. They've been known to do this in other countries, as well.

The Domovoi, the "one of the house" in Slavic cultures, is one of the exceptions to the salt rule in fairyland. He is very pleased when given offerings of bread, beer, and salt. Remember how we said salt is a rare fairy food? Not for the domovoi! We suspect though that this may have to do with his true origins, as he is an ancestor of the family's. And while he may appear to be one of the fae folk, he may truly be an tutelary spirit crossed-over to fae. Remember! He doesn't appreciate foul language at the dinner table and MUST be provided with regular offerings to keep him happy and encourage him to do his duties. Which are protecting the family and house and providing prosperity and health.

Food Offerings to Appease the Fae

If you decide to invite a faery into your home or garden, the first thing you must know is they LOVE offerings of food and drink. Regular offerings, mind you. I don't think our resident Mr. Kobold would have stuck around in our humble abode if it wasn't for the weekly meals, desserts, and libations we've offered over the years. YES, it's like feeding another member of the family! Particularly when it comes to household fairies like kobolds and brownies. If you can't offer regular offerings to your household fae, it might be best to steer clear of inviting one inside. The garden variety of fae require less care and feeding.

Depending on what type of fairy you're honoring will define their preferred offering. Do your research first! We have quite a bit of info on fairy foods and what fairies like to eat here, but it would take an entire book to list all of them. So read and research on your own, too. Just to be safe. You don't want to turn your Scottish brownie into an angry, violent boggart because of the wrong food offerings, now do you?

RULE: NEVER EVER try to catch your fairies in the act of partaking in your offerings! This is a rule across the board in fairyland and will likely anger your fairy. Many will simply take the offering and leave, never to return to your home or garden. While others will be angered and turn into a pesky, sometimes aggressive spirit.

Modern Fairy Cakes and Fairy Bread

Fairies love eating sweets, particularly little cakes, breads, and cookies. But just because something has the word "fairy" before it online, doesn't necessarily mean it's a traditional fairy food or offering. Fairy cakes and fairy bread are two examples of this. Fairy cakes are a smaller British version of the American cupcake. They also don't have buttercream frosting like in the U.S., but more of a glaze icing instead. And much less of it. The cake itself is also a spongier texture than the American cupcake. Do the fairies appreciate a tasty fairy cake of this kind? Absolutely! But it doesn't mean that it was once a traditional fairy food, mind you. In the same breath, any small cake made specifically for the fae is technically a fairy cake!

As for fairy bread, again fairies love baked goods. So any bread you make or provide with intention to them, they'll appreciate. But fairy bread of the modern perception is an Australian concept. It's essentially sliced white bread, coated in copious amounts of butter, and covered in "hundreds and thousands". Or what Americans call sprinkles. It's frequently provided to children at birthday parties. It's truly fun to make!

Herbal Teas for the Fae

Something we've found to appease the fae folk is herbal teas. The garden variety of fae aid in growing herbs so why wouldn't they enjoy drinking an infusion or two? In addition to offering the tea, drink your own cup to aid in visionary journeying to fairyland. Here's a few herbal teas that increase psychic abilities and ease in trance-like meditations:

- Hawthorn leaf and berries
- Thyme
- Rosehip
- Elder flower and berries
- Mugwort
- Wormwood
- Chamomile

- Lavender
- Damiana
- Catnip
- Spearmint

Add a little local honey to your herbal tea. Bees are friends of the faery folk, after all. And honey is an ancient elixir of life. Drink your tea before bed to dream of the fae or receive messages from Elfland in your sleep. Mugwort specifically helps in increasing your dreaming abilities. Always be careful before consuming any herbs…consult with a qualified healthcare provider before starting an herbal regimen as some herbs can interact with medications and with other herbs too! In addition, make sure you don't have an allergy to an herb before consuming an entire cup. Please be careful and ask a professional, ESPECIALLY if you are pregnant or nursing. Herbs like Mugwort can be dangerous to a pregnant or nursing mother.

Household Spirits: How to Feed and Care For Them

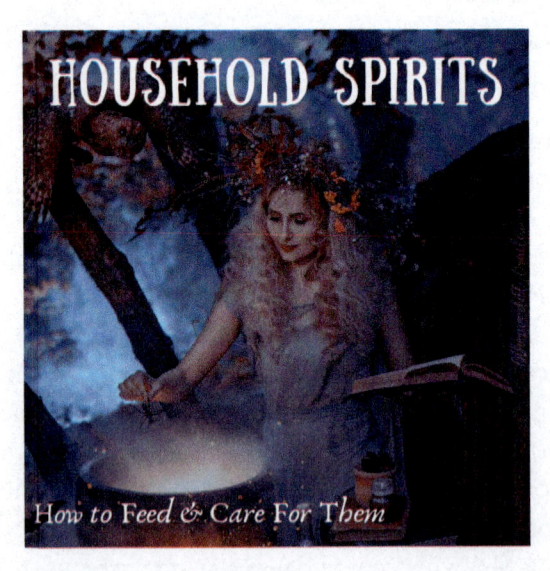

Are you a kitchen or cottage witch who wants an extra helping hand around the house? Maybe you could use some help with your magical workings or someone to protect your household. Household spirits are perfect for the job! Ever heard of the Scottish brownie? The Russian Domovoi? Even if you don't have a gnome or fairy living in your house, you DO have the actual spirit of your house. This spirit can be made into a friend and magical ally. Read on to learn more.

How a House Acquires Its Spirits

Most of our ancient ancestors believed everything in nature had consciousness. When trees were cut down and other things from nature were used to build a home the fairies or spirits linked to these items were brought into the home. Others believed the fairies occupying the landscape where a home was built became household spirits. This is why there were many superstitions as to where a home was built. For example, our Scandinavian ancestors stayed the night at the site of a new home to see if evil spirits manifested. If the person slept peacefully, the home would be built there.

There were different methods of testing a suitable site, including checking the ground or nearby trees for signs of a previous fire. Fire was a bad sign, associated with evil spirits, and many people refrained from building somewhere that had a fire. If there were good fairies on the new home's site, the homeowners petitioned the nature spirits to become their household gods.

Ancestors' Buried in the Hearth

Other methods of acquiring a household spirit were a bit disturbing. In ancient Eastern Europe and parts of Asia, when a new home was built, a person might be sacrificed and buried in the walls or hearth. The victim's spirit was eternally tied to the home and became the household god or guardian. When a family member died a violent death in the home, the windows were opened immediately to let the soul out. They didn't want a violent spirit lingering and wreaking havoc on the household. If a family moved into an already-established home, the original owner of the home would become the household spirit. Ancestors who lived in a house beforehand could also become household spirits. Read about more of these traditions in Claude Lecouteux's book "The Tradition of Household Spirits".

Ancient Roman and Egyptian Household Gods

The ancient Romans honored household gods called Lares. Each household maintained an altar, like the re-created altar shown below. In the richer homes, there was a painting or sculpture to represent the household gods and offerings were left in front. The household gods' images were placed at the dinner table to partake in the family meal. These Roman household gods were guardian spirits who protected the home and the family from illness and invasion.

Lares weren't only household gods in Roman times, they also guarded places in nature. This points to the fact that lares were originally nature spirits brought into the home and deified. Interestingly, the lares were often depicted as snakes (as seen in the painting on the altar here) and lived under the hearth. This points to the idea that perhaps the lares were fire elementals of some kind.

Bes is an ancient Egyptian god who was thought of as a guardian of the common peoples' homes. Many Egyptian families kept altars for Bes and worshiped him. He was invoked to protect the household, provide abundance, and to aid in fertility and childbirth. Interestingly, this Egyptian household god is frequently depicted with holding a snake in his hand. I find this link to snakes and household spirits seemingly stretching across ancient cultures.

How to Care For The Spirit of Your House

First, we'll start with caring for the spirit of your house. Which may be the most important and is neglected by 99% of homeowners (if not more). Your house itself is the physical structure that shields you from outside intrusive forces – weather, intruders, etc. Plus, it serves as a sanctuary for your family. So why not show it some love?

1. Talk to it.

Just by recognizing that your house has a soul is enough to show gratitude. By talking to it, you are acknowledging that it has life. It has consciousness. Tell it about any renovations or changes you plan to make before making them. Put a hand on a wall and thank your house for doing its job. Sounds crazy, but it works. Don't believe me that your house is alive? Ask for confirmation. On one occasion my daughter and I simultaneously saw our house "breathing" (no, we don't have carbon monoxide leaking in our house!)

2. Name your house.

In the old days, every house was given a name. Just like a person. If you travel to the historical parts of the U.S. (and I'm sure elsewhere in Europe, etc.) the older homes all have names. Green Manor. House of the Seven Gables. Oak Manor. Our Lady of Mercy, Etc. This is an ancient tradition that was passed down through the generations that, all until recent years, had continued. You don't have to name your house anything fancy. Even if it's just your last name + manor / estate / mansion, etc.

3. Offerings for Household Spirits

On special occasions, or however often you want, provide offerings to the spirit of your house. This is especially important if renovations are about to begin. Ever hear stories of ghosts and hauntings being stirred up from renovations? I often wonder if this isn't the spirit of the house itself and not necessarily a ghost. Offerings can be anything – water, wine, beer, mead, milk, sweets, a portion of your dinner, etc. When you give the offering, state what it's for and your house will know.

4. A Spell Written by Author Valerie Worth

From Worth's book Crone's Book of Magical Words, A Spell for Pleasing the Household Spirits:

"From a golden broom, pluck five long straws,

Light them as tapers at the fire;

Carry them through the house, and cause

Their subtle smoke to thicken the air—

Then summon good fortune with this spell:

'Wraiths of the house,

Take heart and live:

To every chamber

This light I give,

To every corner

This breath I send—

Approve and favor

My willing hand.'

If you would please them doubly well,

Sprinkle the floor with leaves of tea

And orris powder and grains of salt—

Then sweep with the broom, until you free

Each crack and crevice from speck or fault."

Caring for Household Spirits: The Brownie, Ancestors, Gods, Etc.

In addition to the spirit of your house, you might have other household spirits to feed and care for. I know at my house we have ancestors present in our home, as well as guardians. We should acknowledge their presence, feed, and care for them, as well. Why? Our ancestors, guardians, familiars, gods, etc. protect and watch over us, bring us blessings, and aid in our magical workings when asked. Our relationships with our household spirit should be a two-way street.

1. Feeding Household Spirits

If you have ancestors present in your home, it may be best to set up an altar for them and provide offerings daily or weekly there. This feeds their spirit/energy and shows your gratitude. While ancestors will always protect us, whether we feed/care for them or not, if we do put more effort into our relationship their blessings on us grow ten-fold! As for feeding/caring for household spirits like brownies, domovoi, etc., you'll need to research what offerings they like best traditionally.

2. Room for Brownies, Domovoi, Etc.

Ancestors are typically fond of altars, but brownies and household fairies might prefer their own closed-off space. You can create a "room" for them in a linen closet or some other undisturbed cabinet. Clear off a shelf and put a small pillow, blankets, and other comfy objects there for your brownie/elf to rest. Guardian spirits will take up residence in a doll, statue, or other figure if invited in. Once they've taken up residence in this figure, clean it regularly, dress it in oils, and give offerings to it, as well. The domovoi may prefer sleeping and hiding out in a chimney or old stove. Keep it clean and uncluttered for him/her.

Your Relationship With Household Spirits

The relationship and bond you have with your ancestors, gods, household spirits, etc. is truly in YOUR hands. Just like a relationship with a friend or loved one, it takes care and feeding. It takes time and effort. Don't assume that the spirit of your house, ancestors, or gods will come sweeping in to help you whenever you demand it if you're not putting any effort into the relationship. This means regular communication, offerings/gifts, and just plain acknowledgement of their presence. The more you connect with them, the more they will help you, your magic, and your family!

How to Find a Fairy In Your House

First and foremost, if you want to find a fairy in your house, believe in them. Fairies only show themselves to people who believe OR people who need to learn a lesson. You want to be the believer, not the fairy's student. Secondly, not everyone will have this being in their household, whether you want one or not. The fairy folk don't play by human rules. They have their own.

First, What is a Fairy? And What Isn't?

I find most people's understanding of what a fairy is, well, it just isn't correct. It's incredibly difficult to define these beings. We could take up a few pages discussing the various theories on what a fairy is including land spirits, demonized gods, the ghosts of our ancestors, unbaptized babies doomed to wandering the earth, primitive small-sized humans and many others. We're not going to debate it here. But what I will tell you is this, I believe they are elemental beings…spiritual beings that can manifest in the physical. And I believe they may be attached to the earth, to its forests, mountains, rivers, and such. Sometimes they attach themselves to land, homes that sit on that land, and sometimes to the humans that live there.

I also believe that some fairies are attached to families or bloodlines. They are guardian spirits or guides that are passed down from person to person over the centuries. Sometimes these "fairies" may have even once lived human lives and now they have the job to protect the family's line from the Otherworld. Still sometimes we can summon these beings to us and into our homes. But it takes a special person, the right conditions, and the willing fairy to live in our houses.

What They Aren't

Don't be mistaken. Not all fairies look like Tinkerbell and act like Cinderella's fairy godmother. Many are mischievous, misshapen, and even downright frightening to behold. The garden fairy variety are typically the ones that look closest to the pixie Tinkerbell. But you also have gnomes that take up residence in the roots of old trees that sometimes look endearing, other times creepy. Don't expect that whatever being is in your house will be cute and cuddly. The fae are unpredictable and shapeshifting beings. They aren't to be messed with and they aren't simply play-things.

Signs There Are Fairies In Your House

If you're a friend of the fairies, it's possible you already have a fairy living in your house. You may even live on the land where fairies have always resided. Or you've called one to you through magical endeavors. There are usually a few tell-tale signs when a fairy is already living in your house:

- the cat or dog acts strangely, plays with someone/something invisible or stares up at the ceiling
- food goes missing without explanation, particularly sweets and milk
- strange noises at night: furniture being jumped on, light footsteps on stairs or in hallways, tapping noises in closets and on walls
- doors opening and closing
- chores in your home get done without anyone's knowledge (shouldn't we all be so lucky?!)
- jewelry and sparkly items go missing and turn up in odd or obvious places

- milk or beer goes bad before expiration dates with no explanation
- seemingly poltergeist-like activity (again this depends on the type of fairy in your home)
- new types of plants and vines growing around the outside of your home
- household members' hair is braided or knotted at night in small tight knots (fairy-knots) with no explanation
- finding small objects like dollhouse furniture, doll clothes, etc. around the home or property
- missing keys, remote controllers, shoes, etc. that turn up in odd places

Ancestral Heritage & Fairies

In fairy folklore, the oldest families in Scotland, Ireland, Germany and England have fairies attached to them. Either the fairies guard the property these families own OR the fairies guard the families directly. In Irish folklore, the bean-sidhe (banshee), has shown herself to certain ancient Irish families to warn them of oncoming death or to mourn a current death. The O'Briens, O'Neills, O'Connors, O'Gradys, and Kavanaghs have been haunted by the banshee for centuries. There are similar stories with the Scottish brownies, fairy queens and other fairies. My Scottish ancestors, who descend from the McFee Clan, claim descent from a selkie. It's likely this being may be attached to my bloodline.

How to find a fairy in your house

You have the signs and you know there's a fairy in your home but you can't find it? Fairies are finicky and they follow their own rules. The best thing to do is wait until the fairy is ready and willing to show itself. Most fairies will not come out of hiding – they don't trust human beings. This is from many years of our disbelief, and years of our Christian ancestors calling them evil. Also think of the damage we're doing to the Earth, their sacred place. In addition, folklore says that if you try to "catch" a fairy off guard or while they're doing their business around the house, they will be offended and leave at best. Some stories tell of fairies like the kobold going on an angry rampage, hurting, and even killing those who wronged them. So, my recommendation is this – don't try to "catch" a glimpse of the fairy. Let it come to you, willingly.

Fairy Offerings

Here's the thing. You won't be able to find a fairy in your home because the fairies will only be found if they want to be. Next you can try to coax the fairy out of hiding. Leave a sweet treat as an offering to the fairy on one of the Celtic holy days (fairies are active on May Day, Summer Solstice, and Halloween). Fairy bread, cakes, cupcakes, brownies, and other sweets are favorite fairy foods. Mead, ale, milk, and sweet cream are the fairies' favorite things to drinks.

It takes time.

If you leave offering after offering and nothing happens, it's possible you may never actually see the fairy. Just give him or her time. It's also possible he or she fears a person or animal in your home. Wait until you're by yourself and try talking to the fairy. Give them a hello, let them know you're a friend, and invite them to show themselves when ready. Set up a special place for the fairy, like a shelf in the pantry or linen closet. Or a fairy garden outside.

Things Fairies Dislike

Maybe you've tried everything but still haven't found a fairy in your house. There may be no fairy in your home. There's several things fairies dislike which would prevent them from living in your home.

- Loud, deep-sounding windchimes or bells
- Loud, disobedient children
- Christian/Catholic paraphernalia (crosses, Bibles, etc.)
- Laziness
- Clergymen
- Iron horseshoes, iron skillets, iron tools, etc. (iron traditionally wards off the fae, though I've found this to be different for each type of fairy)
- Bowls of salt (unless you're the Domovoi)
- Noise and commotion
- Lots of clutter
- Stale air
- A home with no whimsy or joy
- People who have no respect for nature
- Being insulted
- People who try to spy on them or catch them in the act

Rid your home of these things – most fairies won't come around for these reasons.

Things Fairies Like in a Home:

- houseplants, trees, and flowers
- shrines and altars to the old gods
- wine cellars and clean, stocked pantries
- herb and flower gardens
- extra cabinet/closet space for them to hide
- fairy altars with offerings
- people with a reverence for nature

- sweet, imaginative children
- people who believe in the fae
- shiny, sparkly things (i.e. jewelry, crystals, etc.)
- water (in bowls or fountains)
- music

The Best Kinds of House Fairies

Just because you're dying for fairy activity in your home doesn't mean to invite all the energy that comes your way. This can be dangerous. You wouldn't go up to a stranger on the street and invite them into your home, would you? It's the same with fairies, they are unpredictable and vary in intent and personality just like humans. Fairies are ancient, otherworldly beings. They don't follow the same moral code humans do.

The Brownie: Scottish House Elf

The best type of fairy to have in your home is the Scottish Brownie. The Brownie is a house fairy or elf and it occupies a deserving Scottish family's home. The Brownie originates in Scotland but is also in North America because of the Scottish immigrants. He's short and stout like a gnome and wears earth colors and sometimes the color red. The Brownie is the best type of fairy to have in your home because he enjoys helping with unfinished chores when the family is asleep. In some legends, Brownies are friends with roosters or even shapeshift into roosters. The rooster's crow in the morning is a warning to the Brownie that daylight is approaching.

Sprites & Pixies in the House and Garden

Sprites and pixies are fairies commonly found in proximity to humans; however, they're not the best type of fairy to have in your home. They're capricious in nature: always getting into trouble and playing little tricks. They like taking jewelry and hiding it in random places, and they'll hide your keys on busy mornings! It's best to keep sprites and pixies in your garden and not in the house. Fairies to watch out for (these fairies are deceitful): goblins/hobgoblins, trolls, ogres, kelpies, any fairy from the Unseelie Court. These fairies are easy to identify – you'll get a sick feeling in their presence. Don't accidentally invite these buggars into your home.

Fairy Knot Magic: A Witch's Ladder

At Beltane, the Green Man returns to the woods bringing fertility and wild growth. The fairies also make their grand return. But if you live in the suburbs or city, how can you attract the Fay if you don't have an innately wild or natural setting close-by? Here we teach our Bella Donna members how to make a witch's ladder to cast fairy knot magic that will attract the Fay to your suburban yard/garden OR city balcony/windowsill.

Make a Witch's Ladder for Your Garden or Window

Fairies love a few things in particular: gardens, wildlife, wilderness, sweets, and shiny things. With that in mind, if you live in the suburbs and have a small garden or yard, you can hang this witch's ladder there. If you live in the city, hanging it from a balcony or in a window will attract the Fay too! Just be careful where you're inviting them in…they are mischievous creatures.

What You'll Need:

- String, ribbon, or twine (2 ft or more – it depends on how long you want to make your witch's ladder)
- Trinkets: small sparkly items to attract the Fay (5 for every other knot you'll make or 9 for every knot)
- Some examples of small trinkets for your fairy knot magic include: seashells, crystal pendants, sun catchers, feathers, bells, beads

How to Make Your Fairy Witch's Ladder

1. Gather all materials and cleanse your space if you choose.

144

2. Turn on whimsical music or nature sounds if you're inside (if you can be outside to make the witch's ladder, even better!)
3. Start by making a knot at one end of the ribbon, while knotting the ribbon say, "By knot of one, my fairy spell has begun" and add your first trinket to the knot.
4. Then moving down the ribbon 3-5 inches approx. Tie a second knot and say, "by know of two, good folk I call on you."
5. Move down another 3-5 inches approx. and tie your next trinket into the third knot and say, "by knot of three, at my garden/windowsill/balcony live free."
6. On the fourth knot, say "by knot of four, ye witch's ladder is your door."
7. On the fifth knot add another trinket, tie, and say, "by knot of five, with your help may my magic thrive."
8. On the sixth knot, tie and say, "may my garden/window/balcony act as your betwixt."
9. On the seventh knot, add another trinket, tie, and say, "by knot of seven, may my garden/window/balcony be a serene, fairy heaven."
10. On the eighth knot, tie and say, "by knot of eight, sweet fairies, come now and don't be late."
11. On the ninth knot, add your last trinket and say, "by knot of nine, my fairy spell is true and divine."
12. Then say, "so be it."
13. Hang your fairy witch's ladder in a tree in your garden, from your balcony or windowsill to attract the Fay.

Fairy Potions: Magical Fay Elixirs for All 4 Seasons

Fairies aren't just dainty little winged creatures that dance from flower-top to flower-top. They are powerful spiritual beings that, with the right mindset and hard work, can aid you in your magical rituals and spells. Healing, dreaming, shapeshifting, and intuition are gifted from the fay to the willing and pure-of-heart. In addition to calling on and using offerings to attract the fay, you can align yourself with fay energy by brewing and drinking fairy potions.

A Quick Warning on the Faery Folk

There seems to be a misconception of what a fairy is versus what Hollywood has taught us. Tinkerbell is cute and fun to watch on the TV screen, but fairies are fickle and sometimes downright dangerous elemental beings. They don't follow the rules of the human world because they aren't of this world. They manifest in the physical but they are truly spiritual entities from the Otherworld (a spiritual realm). The fairies have their own set of rules, of which we are not privy to. So please be careful when reaching out to the fae and don't just call on any fairy to come your way. Research and develop an understanding of the elementals in your area. Learn how to protect yourself while in trance and meditative states, as well as at night during dream work.

What is a fairy potion?

What is a fairy potion? A fairy potion is a cool or hot drink that's intended to align oneself with fairy energy. Typically, fruits, herbs and honey are ingredients used in faery elixirs. This is because many fairies are attracted to certain fruits and herbs that grow in the garden. And honey is a natural sweetener and a product of honeybees (sacred to fairies). It's about getting to know which ingredients have fairy folklore and energy attached. Fairy potions also make great libation offerings to the good folk.

A Winter Solstice Fairy Potion

This recipe is my take on mulled apple cider, perfect for the Winter Solstice and used to attract Winter fairies. But be warned! Not all winter fairies are kind. NO fairy is predictable! Learn how to protect yourself from malevolent fairies here.

Winter Solstice Fairy Potion Ingredients:

- One Cinnamon Stick
- 3 Cups All-Natural Apple Juice
- Allspice 1 tbsp
- 1 cup All-Natural Orange Juice
- 1 teaspoon raw honey
- 1/2 cup Brandy
- 1 tsp jasmine

Directions for the Winter fairy potion:

1. Tie the loose allspice, jasmine, and cinnamon into a piece of cheesecloth or a coffee filter, and drop in a large saucepan along with all the other ingredients (except for the brandy).
2. Bring to a boil and then reduce heat to simmer. Cover and let steep on simmer for about 15 minutes.
3. Take out the spice bag and stir in the brandy. Add a teaspoon of honey to each cup for sweetness. Drink with your coven immediately OR by yourself. FYI Makes enough for half a dozen witches. OR fairies.

Spring Equinox Fairy Potion

Spring is the season for flower fairies, pixies, and the like. If you're heading into nature to search for the fay, drink this herbal tea first:

Spring Fairy Potion Ingredients:

- 1/2 tsp thyme
- 1 tsp elder flower
- 1/2 tsp chamomile
- 1/2 tsp rosebuds
- 1 tsp honey (for sweetening)

Spring Fairy Potion Directions:

1. Steep all herbal ingredients in 8 ounces of hot water for 6 minutes.
2. Remove herbs and add tsp of honey for sweetness.
3. Chant over your cup of tea: "Fairies good and fairies sweet, bless this tea until we meet."
4. Give a little to the fae folk. I like to leave a small cup outside in my garden or on my back step.

A Midsummer Potion to Dance with Faeries

When Midsummer is upon us, the air is heavy and hot; the trees are in bloom. The fairies are dancing and frolicking…just waiting for chosen magical people to join. But as magical people and friends of the fairies, we know that to dance with them with no protection could mean our demise. Legend tells us of many who have gone to dance with the fairies at Midsummer and never return. If you are a strong individual and pure of heart, or if you are a fairy witch, you must spiritually cleanse and protect yourself FIRST before dancing with the fay.

Herbal Berry Smoothie: A Midsummer Fairy Potion Ingredients

- Fresh Local Produce – 1 cup berries (strawberries, blueberries, etc.)
- Organic Skim OR Almond Milk – 1 cup
- Banana – 1/2
- Dried Vervain – 1/4 tsp
- Dried Rosehips – 1/2 tsp
- Fresh Peppermint Leaves – 3
- Four Ice Cubes

Directions:

1. Add all ingredients (except for the peppermint) to a blender. Blend well until mixture is smooth.
2. Pour blended fairy potion into a glass cup, add the three peppermint leaves to the top and gently stir into the smoothie.
3. Enjoy this potion before your Midsummer ritual and before taking to the fields to dance with the faeries.

Note: choose fresh locally grown berries or fruit. During the summer and in my area, we usually find blueberries or blackberries that are organic and locally grown. The fairies will be more attracted to someone who has consumed plants native to their homeland. The reason this fairy potion is chilled is to keep you hydrated before your romp with the fay. Trust me…you'll need it.

4. A Samhain Fairy Potion

The last harvest festival and the end of the Summer is called Samhain (society calls it Halloween). The fairies are busy on Samhain, but be warned! Their disposition turns darker. Samhain is the day when the veil between the our world and the spirit world is thin. Drink this Samhain fairy potion for protection and also to increase psychic abilities. This is the perfect day to practice divination (tarot, runes, etc.) Be sure to cleanse your space and tools first, then cast a circle.

A Samhain Fairy Potion Ingredients:

- 1/2 tsp Mugwort (light sedative and produces prophetic dreams OR astral travel – do NOT take if you are pregnant or nursing)
- 1 tsp Thyme
- 1/2 tsp red hibiscus
- 1 tsp honey
- 8 ounces hot water

Samhain Potion Directions:

1. Make this tea with a tea ball or a loose-leaf tea infuser.
2. Pour hot water over it and the honey and enjoy!
3. Don't forget to ground, center, and shield yourself before drinking this fairy potion and before conversing with the fay ESPECIALLY on Samhain! Ground again after fairy work.

Protection from Trickster Fairies

Fairy protection is sometimes necessary. If you are a friend of the fay like me, you've seen their beauty and wonder. They might have helped your garden grow or give you a healing remedy in your dreams. You've seen the good that fairies do for Mother Earth; however, occasionally, you may run into a fairy that's not so nice. The reasons for their distrust towards us are many-fold, but the main thing is to learn how to protect yourself from trickster fairies.

First, Are There Really "Evil Fairies"?

Well, are there bad spirits? Bad human beings? When you start working with the fairy realm, you'll quickly realize not all fairies are friendly to humans. In fact, there are some that kidnap and eat humans according to folklore. While others may not be particularly cannibalistic but tend to play tricks on their human encounters. In addition, there are household fairies that may first be friendly and helpful that turn malevolent or angry for one reason or another. There are even fairies, namely the will o' the wisp, that are known to lead human beings off a cliff and to their tragic end.

But, to answer the question are there evil fairies, understand the faery realm follows its own rules. So, what we find "evil" isn't one thing or another in the faery realm. Still, there are some who enjoy working and living alongside humankind.

Fairy Protection: Ways to Protect Your Home & Yourself

Fairy protection dates back thousands of years and consists of many different practices. If you are working with fairies in your magickal practice or trying to attract them to your home or garden, these methods of protection should not scare the benevolent fairies away. These methods of fairy protection should only keep potentially malevolent fairies from your home if your intention is pure.

1. Iron Protection from Malevolent Fairies

It's been said for centuries that fairies fear iron, hang an iron horseshoe above your front door to ward off evil fairies. This belief could be due to the idea that fairies were originally a small neolithic people who lived in Ireland and were driven out of their homes by the Celts, specifically in the Iron Age (hence the fear of iron – iron weapons). Cast iron in the kitchen protects from trickster fae spoiling or overturning food. Wearing an iron troll cross, like the kind they wear in Sweden, wards off evil elves, trolls, and the like. Or hang iron troll crosses around the home and garden.

2. Bells and Chimes

Bells frightened off evil spirits in Medieval Ireland and elsewhere in Europe. Specifically, the big, deep-sounding Church bells that would ring to draw the people to Church. Apply this tradition by hanging deep-toned chimes on your front porch, or by using deep sounding bells during magickal ritual. Use bells to clear your space should there be trickster spirits about.

3. Protection from Fairy Raids and Rings

If going out walking at night or during twilight hours, or if you go out on one of the eight holy days, it's imperative to protect yourself from getting caught up in one of the fairies raides (rides) or fairy rings. Old Irish folklore says that one is to turn their coat inside out to keep from being "pixie-led" away from a safe path. Also, NEVER take food from the fay! If you are caught in a fairy ride or ring, or if you take food from the fay, you could very well find yourself lost in a strange place. When you return, YEARS could have gone by even though it only felt like minutes (according to folklore).

4. Don't Traipse Into Their Territory

The easiest way to prevent getting caught in a fairy raid or being dragged to the depths of a pond is simple. Stay out of their way. Stay out of their territory. Most people can feel when they're teetering closely to the Otherworld or a company of fairies. You'll hear harp or flute music, seemingly far away yet close by. And the world around you will seem to shift. Or feel unstable. There are sometimes known fairy haunts in certain places throughout the world. It's best to leave these places alone. If you happen to enter their territory unbeknownst to you, tell them you mean no harm and leave promptly.

5. Appeasing the Fay

Leave a pail of fresh milk, butter, or cream outside of your front door on the eight holy days to appease the fay and keep them from wreaking havoc on garden and home. Leaving fairy offerings and libations dates back hundreds of years, and if you have any Celtic ancestors, you probably have ancestors who partook in this tradition. Some people in Europe still do! This is a preventative method of protection from trickster fairies. Make them happy at the back door so they don't intrude. Fairies are also particularly active in the days leading up to Samhain and during the Twelve Days of Yule.

6. The Circle of Light

Another effective yet simple technique of fairy protection consists of using one's mind and energy. If you are used to using visualization in your meditations, rituals, and spells, this method of fairy protection should be familiar to you. It's what I like to call the Circle of Light. You can do this visualization exercise any time of the day, any day of the week and as often as you'd like. For me particularly, I do it every night as I'm lying in bed and before I go to sleep to continue to build the circle's strength around my home.

Circle of Light Visualization Tutorial

Just relax your entire body. Let all thoughts and chatter of your mind fade away until all your picture is a blank screen. Then see your home and property on the screen, see its colors and details. Focus on the image of your home and property, then look in the window at yourself and/or your family members. Then gradually picture a circle of white light engulfing your home, starting from the ground, and going up and over, forming a dome of light. See this light as being transparent, but totally impenetrable by negative forces. Picture a branch or rock being thrown at the dome of light and watch it bounce off. Then picture an evil fairy trying to cross the circle of light's boundary and watch them be pushed away. Repeat this visualization technique every night for at least a week, and then repeat whenever you feel necessary.

7. Ancestral and Deity Protection from Malevolent Fairies

One of the MOST effective forms of protection against trickster fairies (and other spirits in general) is to invite your ancestors and gods into your home. Once your guides and guardians take up residence in your home, they do most of the work of keeping out negative forces like malevolent fairies and the like. In fact, my ancestors are SO good at protection, I must ask their permission to allow any other spirits inside the home.

8. Warding Your Property

Warding your property is an effective way to shield yourself and your family from pretty much every spirit you don't want intruding. Except the ones you invite in. This is an effective way to ward off malevolent fairies, as well. Essentially, a circle of salt will ward off fairies, railroad spikes in the four corners of your property, as well as certain stones that contain iron like hematite and red jasper. Another tip – if you choose to use a circle of salt, Himalayan pink salt is even more effective than regular. Why? It has the largest amount of iron…which is what gives it its pink color.

9. Avoiding Travel On Their Days

It's well-known through Ireland and other old countries that the fae are more active on certain days, nights, and holidays during the year. Some of those days include the high Celtic holy days Imbolc, Beltane, Lughnasadh, and Samhain. But if you travel further Northeast in Europe to Norway and Sweden, the elves are quite active during the Winter holidays of Yule and during the 12 days of Christmas. And no, I don't necessarily mean Santa's cute, toy-making elves. I'm talking the danger, sometimes malevolent Alfar. During these days, it's best to avoid traveling on roads by yourself during twilight hours and at night. Lest you stumble upon them and be swept away.

Bibliography

Fields, K. (2023, May 10). Retrieved from Otherworldly Oracle: https://otherworldlyoracle.com

Green, E. L. (2004). *Meeting the Other Crowd: The Fairy Stories of Hidden Ireland.* TarcherPerigee.

Illes, J. (2009). *Encyclopedia of Spirits: The Ultimate Guide to the Magic of Saints, Angels, Fairies, Demons and Ghosts.* HarperOne.

Illes, J. (2014). *Encyclopedia of Witchcraft: The Complete A-Z for the Entire Magical World (Witchcraft and Spells).* HarperOne.

Lecouteux, C. (2013). *The Tradition of Household Spirits: Ancestral Lore and Practices.* Inner Traditions.

Matthews, J. (1998). *Tales of the Celtic Otherworld.* Blanford PR.

McCoy, E. (2002). *A Witch's Guide to Faery Folk: How to Work With the Elemental World.* LLewellyn's Publications.

Worth, V. (2000). *Crone's Book of Magical Words.* St. Paul: Llewellyn Publications.

Yeats, W. (2020). *Fairy and Folk Tales of the Irish Peasantry.*

Printed in Great Britain
by Amazon